Fibromyalgia

At Close Quarters

Author

Barry Hardy

I live in a magnificent body now that I know how to support its needs

Fibromyalgia At Close Quarters

The pre launch version of this book was published 06th February 2009 in Great Britain with First Edition published 20th February 2009.

ISBN 978-0-9559865-7-4

Discover more at www.barryhardy.com

DECENCY WARNING

Please note that Fibromyalgia At Close Quarters contains strong, explicit views including the use of offensive language, which some may find unnecessarily gratuitous. Therefore please don't read this book if you are easily offended by:

- Strong views.
- Strong language.
- Grammatical inconsistencies.

Or

- Personal experiences and perceptions expressed freely.

DEDICATION

This book is dedicated to the battalions of helpless souls butchered in the killing fields of medical man. We who survive will do our level best to right their wrongs. *Fibromyalgia at Closes Quarters was written and complied entirely in a multicultural internet café in south London and I thank my hosts profoundly for their unequivocal generosity and continued support of my endeavors on this front.*

At the point I began to understand my pain I knew my life had changed

DISCLAIMER

The information provided in this book should not be construed as personal medical or clinical advice or instruction no action should be taken based solely on the contents of this book. Readers should consult appropriate professionals on any matter relating to their health and well being. The information and opinions provided here are for personal research purposes only. Readers who fail to consult appropriate professionals assume the risk of incurring injury and must accept any consequences directly or indirectly associated with their personal actions on any and all related matters.

FOREWORD

Chronic Fibromyalgia is real and what's more it's truly an insidious condition that invades and destroys every aspect of everything that we as mortals, should care to value. It erodes our sense of self, our sense of hope; in fact it erodes the very essence of living a happy, fulfilled and productive life. I know only too well the sheer hell that is; undiagnosed chronic illness including the heavy load it imposes upon our lives. You see, I had an unqualified disease over a 30+ year period that pushed me into a state of chronic illness, fatigue and depression that was beyond belief, so dreadful and so black that the thought of release through death was my only yet constant companion. Today I often wonder just how it was that I was brave enough, strong enough and pragmatic enough to solve the mystery of that condition. Whilst those charged with the responsibility of aiding and helping me, simply sat back on their ignorant behinds or placed the blame for my condition back onto me. Unsurprising really when all things are considered, because the plain fact of the matter is that the medical industry by default, despite any and all protestations to the contrary, simply doesn't understand chronic illness and simply doesn't care about anyone in its care. The result of which is that it is us as that industries employers, who inevitably suffer as a result of all its mortal failings, prejudices, scientific ignorance and underperformance on a global scale. To fully understand the sheer depths of suffering that I

At the point I began to understand my pain I knew my life had changed

endured to acquire myself healing and self management knowledge you should perhaps read my foundation book *Raphael's Legacy published in 2008*. For in that book I cover many aspects of my own personal pursuit of well being as well as publicly denouncing the fraudulent myth's and prejudices within our medical model that result in so much misdiagnosis and medical/clinical underperformance on a global scale. Before we go any further together on this journey I need to make you clear about one very important point; you see, although I find myself writing this self help book. Actually I have absolutely no medical qualifications and/or medical training; however I do have enough intellect and chronic illness expression experience to be eminently qualified enough to voice my opinions upon how to investigate, treat and remove from our lives what is an indiscriminately cancerous condition. You see, chronic illness expression in the vast majority of instances does not originate from insanity or emotional instability despite;

- Any and all claims by the medical/clinical industry that they are the only true generators of the chronic illness expression.

Or

- Any and all current or formative neuro-linguistic programming that reinforces the point that insanity or emotional instability are the only true generators of the chronic illness expression.

Because

- Only bodily disease, bodily system/process failures, issues with your endocrine system or chronic inflammation can propagate, promote and / or generate symptoms of chronic illness expression and that as far as I am concerned is FACT.

ACKNOWLEDGMENTS

My sincere thanks go out to:

My lovely Karina without who's love and support for and of me there would have been no mortal redemption or hope for me.

Dr Sarah Myhill and Hania Baker for all their support and generosity towards my wellbeing and clinical care.

Mrs Edna Garrick for her generosity in agreeing to proof read my manuscript for me.

Mr Abdi Nur Ali, Mr. Dahir Nur Ali and Mr Abdikarin Mohamed for their generosity during the compilation of this book in their internet café on Westow Hill.

Finally to all the medical / clinical incompetents that I've encountered thus far, you are the only reason for this books production. I always knew that there was an answer to my problem and having proved that I'm now happy to share it with the world.

At the point I began to understand my pain I knew my life had changed

ESSENTIAL READING

Everything covered in this book draws upon my own detailed personal passage through chronic illness that I cover in my book *Raphael's Legacy*. To ensure that you understand and / or do not either misinterpret or misrepresent any statement, phrase or passage in this book, please ensure that you have read Raphael's Legacy prior to exploring the subtle nuances of this book. In that way you can ensure that you fully understand why I say the things I say and why I propose the things in the way that I propose them in this book. For your reference a listing of all Raphael's Legacy derivative support books are at your disposal on the next page. Finally and above all things, please ensure that as you move towards better health always ensure that you are adequately supported by a suitably qualified professional service provider.

I live every day to the full now since I began to live again pain free

Further personal insight and self help books written by Barry Hardy in relation to Raphael's Legacy include:

Raphael Treatment Protocol
Stress at Close Quarters
Anxiety at Close Quarters
Exploring Fluid Normality
Arthritis at Close Quarters
Depression at Close Quarters
Lymes Disease at Close Quarters
Manic Depression at Close Quarters
Gulf War Syndrome at Close Quarters
Toxic Body Syndrome at Close Quarters
Myalgic Encephalopathy at Close Quarters
Chronic Fatigue Syndrome at Close Quarters
Obsessive Compulsive Disorder at Close Quarters

You can purchase any of these books at www.barryhardy.com

CONTENTS

Decency warning 3

Dedication.. 4

Disclaimer.. 5

Foreword.. 6

Acknowledgments.. 8

Essential reading 9

Contents 11

Exploration introduction 13

Exploration of clinical chronic fibromyalgia..................................... 21

Exploring the journey into darkness pragmatically 25

Exploring the darker side of medicine pragmatically 37

Exploring psychological illness pragmatically 45

Exploring lymes disease pragmatically 61

Exploring the thyroid link pragmatically 73

Exploring genetic time bomb links pragmatically 85

Exploring toxic body syndrome... 97

I live every day to the full now since I began to live again pain free

Exploring arthritis pragmatically 111

Exploring fibromyalgia pragmatically 123

Exploring personal mind anger pragmatically 135

Exploring analytical testing pragmatically 143

Exploring analytical testing options pragmatically 165

Exploring your current diagnosis pragmatically 171

Authors notes 185

Web sites you may wish to explore 191

Other books by barry hardy 192

Decency Warning.. 193

At the point I began to understand my pain I knew my life had changed

EXPLORATION INTRODUCTION

Exploration One

I live every day to the full now since I began to live again pain free

At the point I began to understand my pain I knew my life had changed

If you're currently suffering from and/or have suffered from Chronic Fibromyalgia in the past and wish to unravel the truth about everything associated with that expression of disease. Then perhaps it's understandable why you arrived at your decision to read this book. But what you may not know yet is, this book like all my self help books is based upon my own personal approach to illness expression on the firm understanding that I'm certainly no guru or medically/clinically qualified individual. I'm just a regular guy who ignored my doubters and abusers and took my conditions head on until I was able to qualify my conditions root cause via scientific analysis. Therefore if you're interested in exploring my views all I would ask is that you:

(a) Stay open and consider fully any and all of the postulations I explore in this book for the pursuit of well-being, before deciding upon the most appropriate approach or course of action for you.

And

(b) Always work with or at least consult with; a suitably qualified service provider before making changes to any or all of your current treatment protocols.

Let's not beat around the bush then; as I'm sure you're aware Chronic Fibromyalgia is such an invasive state of existence, for when you are in its grasp, nothing makes sense and all seems to be pain, for in that place you live a life which seems void of hope. But the reality is that where there is life, there is always hope, for where there is hope, there is always the potential for renewal and growth. The essence of my personal renewal and growth was nothing more than tenacity in the midst of seemingly insurmountable odds. Bolstered only by a desire to prove my

I live every day to the full now since I began to live again pain free

antagonists wrong and to reduce where possible the struggle or struggles of any of my fellow men. I believe that; 'anything and everything is possible with the right skills, the right people and the right approach' and in that mind set I proved how to rid myself of chronic illness. During that process I learned who failed me and why they failed me, who chose to ignore me and why they chose to ignore me, but I also learned who truly loved me with all their heart and why they loved me with all their heart and that is the true beauty of success over intense adversity. We all have the potential to recover from chronic illness, no matter what form it takes e.g. Chronic Fibromyalgia. That is if we're truly prepared to accept that we can recover, but if we choose not to recover from chronic illness then we make that choice for the personal reasons that only we know best. I made a firm choice to recover from chronic illness expression and in compiling this book I'm now offering you the tools, understanding and insight to recover from your own chronic condition too i.e. Chronic Fibromyalgia. In committing to my own personal recovery I explored many many things and that's why it's easy for me to acknowledge and pronounce out loud that:

- To those who failed me, who criticised me, who ridiculed me, to those who misdiagnosed me, who mistreated me and who clinically abused me I say to you now: may your god forgive you for all that you are for you are without doubt the lowest of all mortal life forms.

At the point I began to understand my pain I knew my life had changed

- To those who could have, should have, yet chose not to heed me, to help me, to support me or to love me I say to you now, do not attempt to re-write my past by reaching out and connecting with me now or in the future. It's not for me to forgive you your prejudices, your ignorance, your selfishness or your cruelty towards me. As a mortal I merely wish for you strength, growth and rebirth as you pass through your own personal hells that I believe lay before you.

- To those who loved me, who prayed for me, who laughed with me, who cried with me and to those who died with me many times I say to you now; we may be few, but we are the luckiest of all living things. We have loved, we have cared, we have given, we have shared, we have lived and we will die touched by the presence of unquestionable friends.

I firmly believe that you as a sufferer of Chronic Fibromyalgia need to look at the bit and big players in your life for in doing so you will allow yourself to move forward quicker than you ever thought possible. You see; the process to wellness starts completely with a considered acceptance of your past in unison with you future expectations because that and only that approach to life brings forth new ways of being, new ways of thinking and implicitly new ways of living. A life filled with fun and free from manufactured fear or ignorantly propagated prejudices or misrepresentation of scientific fact. Because the very simple FACT is that Chronic Fibromyalgia always originates from:

    1.   Physical diseases and/or rarely injury to the brain.

Or

I live every day to the full now since I began to live again pain free

2. Bodily process failure and/or deviations from normal functioning.

Or

3. Inflammation generated through diseases or injury.

Or

4. Toxic body syndrome generated through, physical disease, bodily process failure and/or deviations from normal functioning and Inflammation generated through diseases or injury.

Now I realise that the points I've made thus far may be a lot for anyone suffering from chronic illness in whatever form that takes to come to terms initially given the general level of perceptional and medical/clinical clap trap surrounding chronic illness. All I can say is that you the reader will always be able to validate or disregard my postulations in relation to your particular illness at the point you've given due consideration to all I have to say. Living with any form of chronic illness is neither right, nor acceptable in any way shape or form and at the point you're free from its deadly expression in your lives, you will again realise why mortality can be such an enriching and simply mind blowing undertaking. I hope that this book changes your views upon Chronic Fibromyalgia, because unlike any other book on Chronic Fibromyalgia. This book will postulate alternative slants on aspects of chronic illness generation, hence opening up new ways of thought, new ways of seeing and new ways of dealing with your Chronic Fibromyalgia. Because once we have at our disposal all the information we need to secure better health, the entire picture and road to recovery becomes so much clearer.

I live every day to the full now since I began to live again pain free

You see, we all have the power to take control of our lives and to live in the way that we choose to live. For in committing to that way of being we are actually setting ourselves free of any of the negative programming we've inherited that has played a big part in compromising our perceptions upon life. We have the right to be all that we were ever born to be, and that means being free always from disease and ignorant prejudices about disease which in reality only hold us back.

On that very point I now invite you to explore my thoughts, views and suggestions designed to eradicate Chronic Fibromyalgia from your lives and sincerely hope at the very least they open up a new avenue of hope for you.

At the point I began to understand my pain I knew my life had changed

EXPLORATION OF CLINICAL CHRONIC FIBROMYALGIA

Exploration Two

At the point I began to understand my pain I knew my life had changed

What is there to say about Chronic Fibromyalgia save for the fact that anyone who suffers from it knows truly just how difficult morality can be. Because sufferers of Chronic Fibromyalgia somehow have to come to terms with chronic and unrelenting anxiety, depression, pain and/or an inability to simply cope, which impact upon the normality of mortality in every way shape and form. Chronic Fibromyalgia, saps resolve and pushes it's sufferers to and beyond seemingly unimaginable points of despair. But the worst thing of all is that populist and medical/clinical perceptions of Chronic Fibromyalgia is; that it's somehow just a manifestation of deep seated psychological and/or psychiatric issues.

But actually I find the perception of Chronic Fibromyalgia strange to say the very least because when you think about it or ask anyone from the medical/clinical world. No one is actually able or prepared to qualify actually what Chronic Fibromyalgia is, over and above that is the bog standard clap trap we've all heard so many times about our psychology being able to manifest disease in all shapes and forms and when we sort our head out, hooray we become Chronic Fibromyalgia free. Well the plain and simple fact of that matter is that Chronic Fibromyalgia is a disease generated symptom, therefore if we wish to make any improvement we need to:

(a) Identify which disease is generating the manifestation of Chronic Fibromyalgia symptomology.

And

(b) Develop a holistic treatment protocol where eradication and not suppression of symptomology remains key.

I live every day to the full now since I began to live again pain free

I'm now going to explore a whole raft of issues which I hope stimulate insight for you, because I actually believe that it's eminently possible to solve personal Chronic Fibromyalgia battles when our search for the truth remains firmly focused upon root cause analysis. With that position very much to the fore, I'm going to cover aspects of my healing process against horrendous odds whilst also hopefully enlightening you on some or the more darker sides of medical/clinical failures of due diligence.

At the point I began to understand my pain I knew my life had changed

EXPLORING THE JOURNEY INTO DARKNESS PRAGMATICALLY

Exploration Three

I live every day to the full now since I began to live again pain free

At the point I began to understand my pain I knew my life had changed

My decline into chronic ill health and intense chronic illness expression resulted from over three decades of medical/clinical abuse and neglect and you can read more about that in my book *Raphael's Legacy*. Nevertheless as a guy who's been through a horrific state of undiagnosed disease I realise now that the fall from good health into that of a chronic diseased state is not always a straight forward process and can take many years. The thing is we have nothing without good health, no prosperity, no career or joy, yet good health is something we all take for granted until it's ripped forever from our grasp. As a society we're not programmed to explore and look for answers when our health is in decline, because we absolve ourselves of that responsibility and empower only a select few. Therein we lose the connection that we need to plot and determine the origin and cause of our disease because as our body's sole custodian we ultimately hold all the answers and that is the only true key to recovery. As part of the foundation work required to support my diseased state postulation it was important for me in the preparation of my book *Raphael's Legacy* that I mapped and shared with you my own personal health decline, for in that process all the connections are clearly defined. With a simple red line mapping depression expression, a blue line mapping physical strength and green line mapping my emotional strength over an entire forty year period.

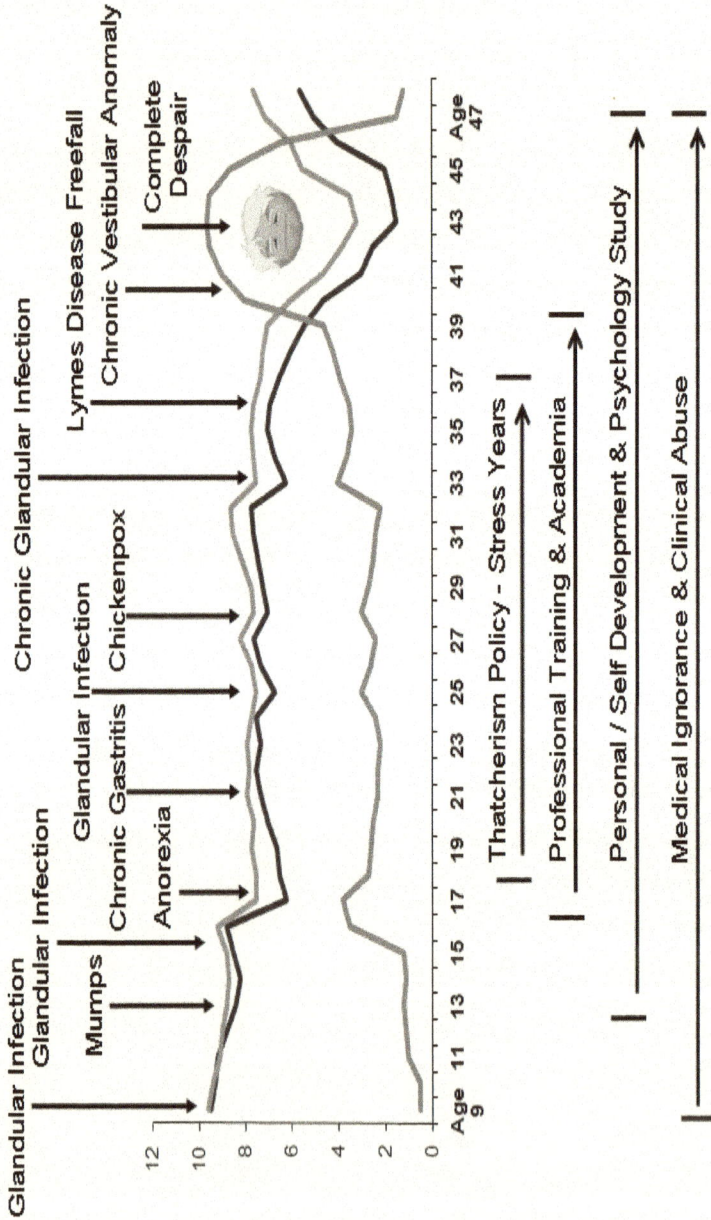

At the point I began to understand my pain I knew my life had changed

Before I elaborate further upon my own health decline however it's important that I cover emotional and depressive state perceptions because they are frequently cited by medical charlatans as the originators of illness. When in reality they are nothing more than an expression of disease. Nevertheless there is a big difference between emotional state and depressive state and they must never be confused or directly linked as one in the same because they are not, *but I will qualify this point further in subsequent chapters.* Our emotional state in essence is our ability to cope, to rise to a challenge, to pick ourselves up after a set back and/or to project ourselves into the future and is nothing more than a derivative of our endocrine functionality.

Whereas depression I'm prepared to argue is nothing more than a symptom of disease and should not therefore be confused with subtle mood swings which are part of our normal emotional expressions. As you will observe my health profile map starts way back at the point of formalized body awareness for me where I'm aware that I had exceptionally high levels of physical endurance and emotional strength with low depression intent i.e. I simply coped, laughed and joked. Those expressions are mapped such that, physical and emotional scores at ten indicate high energy levels and equally very strong emotional stability. Whereas zero would indicate that I have no energy, no resilience, no emotional rigidity, no fight, in essence I'm simply burnt out. In terms of depression expression, zero on the map indicates no depression present whereas ten would indicate chronic suicidal depression. As my health declined it's easy to see the correlation between physical strength and emotional strength and the impact that disease has upon all three states i.e. physical and emotional states decline in vitality and depression increases with paradoxical ferocity during chronic disease. Therefore my primary postulation is that the vast majority of depressive states are a direct result of a diseased state and that depression is not the generator of illness as most medics would have us believe. Depression in itself is not an illness in the vast majority of cases; rather it is merely a symptom that simply manifests through disease. Equally; psychological stress is not the originator of fatigue at best it is merely a bit player or derivative of the same diseased state. It is therefore very important that we all understand that the originator of chronic symptomology is not the fault of the patient it is nothing more than an indicator of disease. Understand that and you're at least part of the way to accepting that you have a condition in Chronic Fibromyalgia which needs treating and that you're not the entire cause of all your presenting symptoms.

In the absence of medical/clinical scientific intellect, my battle for resolution from chronic illness expression took me to places where I would hope no fellow mortal should ever have to go. It cost me my career, my prosperity, my homes and ultimately could have cost me my life had I not been blessed with a little bit of luck and a body and mind that refused to be written off. After three decades of suffering and at a cost of over 300k I was diagnosed with Lyme's Disease, but that process despite all the self sacrifice it required on a physical, emotional, spiritual and financial level, gave birth to a man who now knows:

1. The truth about our medical/clinical industry, all it's failing, ignorance and lack of scientific validity!

And

2. What is needed on the part of any mortal to get well from a whole host of hitherto so called untreatable or so called psychological conditions!

At the point I began to understand my pain I knew my life had changed

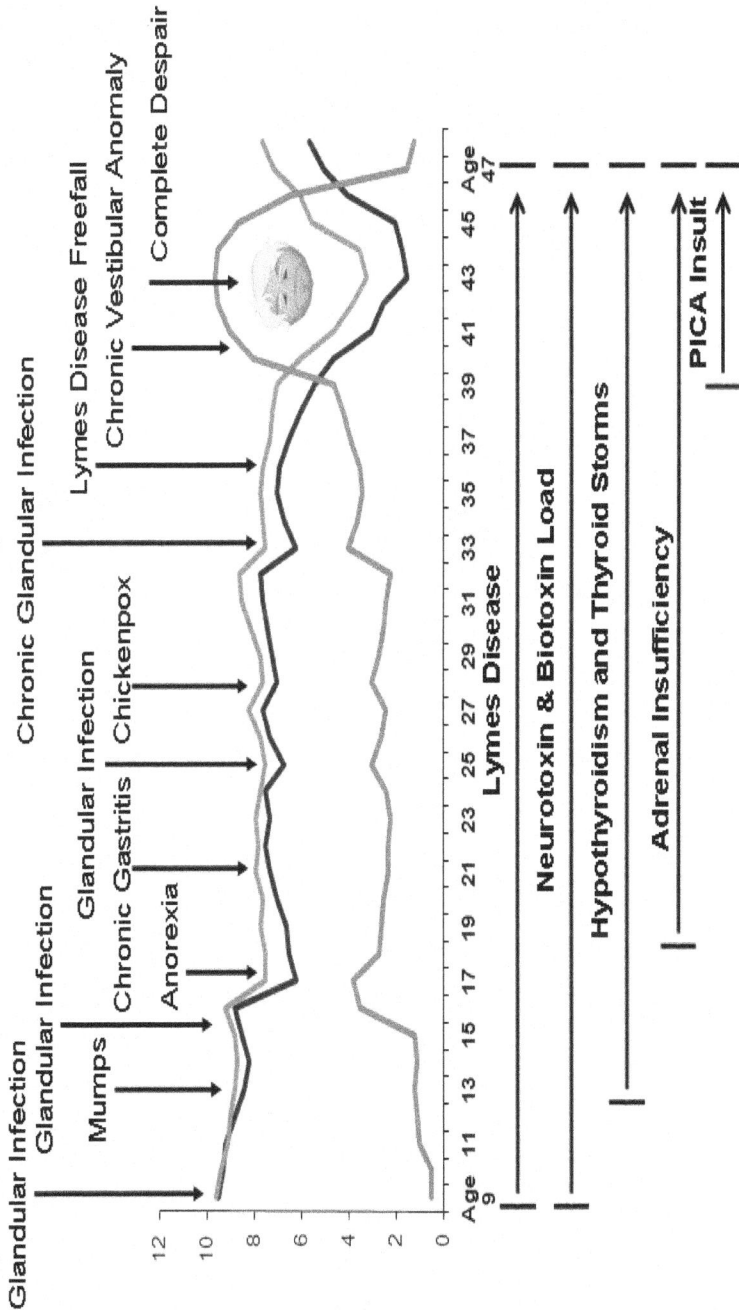

I live every day to the full now since I began to live again pain free

In pursuit of my own personal well being I discovered that:

- I contacted Lymes Disease at a very young age the impact of which was that it compromised my liver, my brain and my endocrine system re: *Raphael's Legacy*

- My bodily systems were simply unable to cope with that untreated load and so over the years battling to solve my body's infection, my body simply burnt itself out, re: *Raphael's Legacy*

- When exposed to even higher levels of Lymes Disease my limited defenses were simply overrun and my health simply went into freefall and I moved very quickly into a rampant Lymes Diseased state and toxic body syndrome, re: *Raphael's Legacy*

- A situation compounded still further by the chronic activation of a simply horrendous vascular vestibular insult which was completely poo poo'd by the medical / clinical charlatans that I saw until I was able to prove its origin via self-funded imaging and neurosurgery re: *Raphael's Legacy*.

At the point I began to understand my pain I knew my life had changed

Now the question is;

Are you open enough, ready enough and / or willing enough to explore your own chronic illness state of Chronic Fibromyalgia from a whole new perspective in an attempt to move both it and you into a new holistic place of considered and greater understanding?

If so;

Then take a deep breath and prepare for a bumpy yet hopefully rewarding ride, because some of the material I'm going to cover from now on in this book may simply shock you to your core.

But hey:

That's okay and I'm sure you'll agree otherwise you wouldn't be reading this book right now would you?

What you may ask has all this got to do with Chronic Fibromyalgia? Well the answer is, not one single medic or clinician helped me when I was being destroyed by a horrendous disease despite that fact that my chronic illness levels were as chronic as it's possible to be. All they ever did was write me off at worst and at best offer me, medications that offered no resolution or hope for me. The plain disagreeable fact of the matter is that there are no medics or clinicians out there who remotely understand disease or Chronic Fibromyalgia which means that we're completely devoid of help at the point our body moves into a chronic diseased state. What's even worse is that by the time our bodies decline into a chronic diseased state the root cause of our disease on our records is so hidden or masked by psychological inaccuracies or simply medical clap trap that the possibility of securing an effective diagnosis is in reality highly remote. I know of far too many people myself included who've been tortured by disease and ultimately chronic illness expression who've been ignored and abused wholesale by the medical/clinical world through dogma, ignorance and incompetence in terms of trying to find a scientific solution to our disease state conditions, to such an extent that it's an absolute bloody scandal. A situation which directly forced me to explore why it was that the medical/clinical world was so reluctant to help people in despair and what needed to change to bring about greater receptivity.

At the point I began to understand my pain I knew my life had changed

During my endeavours on this matter I found only to my great annoyance that the medical/clinical industries including everyone who either works in it or supports it are simply:

- Happy with underperformance and shoddy service delivery.

- Happy to continually write its customer base off whilst continuously seeking to self elevate its/their own status through bullshit and medical/clinical ignorance and dogma.

It is an industry;

- So locked in inertia that its own scientific base is at least one hundred years ahead of its own front end service provision.

Now I'm in no way saying that in order to recover from Chronic Fibromyalgia we all must plot our decline in health similar to the detail that I myself was forced to do so, to enable me to pass though my horrendous and deep black hole. But what I am saying is that there is a need for a significant change in our perceptions about the way we currently perceive poor health and in particular Chronic Fibromyalgia because without that; there is very little potential for symptom free resolution and long term recovery. Therefore the key to freedom from self destruct or medical/clinical abuse in terms of Chronic Fibromyalgia is to always remember that chronic illness expression no matter what form it takes is always the result of anyone or all of the following:

1. Physical diseases.
2. Rarely injury to the brain.
3. Bodily process failure and/or deviations from normal functioning.
4. Inflammation generated through diseases.
5. Inflammation generated through injury to the brain.
6. Toxic body syndrome generated through, physical disease, bodily process failure and/or deviations from normal functioning and inflammation generated through diseases or injury.

EXPLORING THE DARKER SIDE OF MEDICINE PRAGMATICALLY

Exploration Four

I live every day to the full now since I began to live again pain free

At the point I began to understand my pain I knew my life had changed

You may be surprised to read this, but let me send a shock wave racing right through your body because I'm going to empower you with a very distasteful truth. You see, at the point you move into a state of chronic ill health and/or Chronic Fibromyalgia the deadliest people you will ever meet are those who work within and/or who support the medical/clinical world.

So much so that I'm somewhat embarrassed these days by the fact that whilst many turned their back during the greedy and wasted Thatcher and Major years. I spent a great deal of my youth campaigning and lobbying against local and central government with passion on a whole host of issues, not least to save what I felt was a laudable institution under threat, namely our glorious NHS. 'Boy did I get it wrong'. The institution and all the mechanisms that underpin that bullshit ridden and sedentary industry are rotten to the core.

Fortunately I have no medical or clinical qualifications, I'm just a regular guy trained in engineering and engineering sciences and like most engineers I have an engaging and problem solving mind. As a regular guy, albeit with a little bit of professional training, I would respectfully suggest that having an enquiring, capable and problem solving mind is probably the most rudimentary of all mandatory requirements for all those engaged in a key service delivery profession such as the medical industry. Now clearly the back room girls and boys of that industry appear to have that predisposition because we have all witnessed the tremendous advances that have been achieved over the past fifty years or so. I'm talking here however about medical scientists and scientific medical engineers, the people we should regard as the true heroes of medicine, the men and woman who steadfastly develop new tools, new tests, new treatments, new techniques and new machines etc, for the betterment of man. However, the heroes of medicine are a stark contrast to the front end 'luddites' i.e. *Any Opponent of Industrial Change or Innovation* of the medical world that we the general public are unfortunately exposed to. The people that we're exposed to are only interested in one thing and one thing only: self gratification at the expense of their fellow man. I refer of course to the medical receptionist, the nurse, the general practitioner, the registrar, the specialist and the consultant. They may or may not start off life as self protectionist 'luddites' but at the point they're allowed to administer their own unique brand of divisive, destructive and judgmental clinical administration and medical butchery up the innocent public, they move into that 'luddite' mindset wholesale.

These people are guilty of crimes against humanity that simply eclipse the acts and transgressions of the worst of all ruthless dictators. They are institutionally lazy, self obsessed, greedy, serial abusers with only one thing on their agenda, self preservation of their highly inflated status within what is the devil's own institutions. Forget any waffle about the Hippocratic oath that anyone from this industry chooses to offload onto you, the bottom line for these people is themselves first, themselves second and whatever is left over; is all for themselves. These people don't solve problems, they don't hear suffering, they're not prepared to think outside of the box and why? Well because they're the wrong people for the job, the wrong people who are gaining great rewards from an industry that is rotten to the core. For anyone misfortunate enough to develop a Chronic Fibromyalgia I've mapped the actual clinical abuse process that most people are forced to endure during the course of their chronic illness at the end of this chapter. What the process loop cannot do is qualify the simply appalling nature, neglect and abandonment anyone experiences during that process. Where the cause of desperate conditions are often written off as psychological issues and

At the point I began to understand my pain I knew my life had changed

placed directly back on the shoulders of the patients, identifying them as the originator and hence owner of the condition in totality. That being said; it's eminently justifiable to suggest that the selection criteria for individuals entering the medical industry and the training they undergo are now by modern day standards both outdated and fundamentally flawed. Because if the selection criteria for those entering the medical industry and their subsequent training were right; then we wouldn't have such a fundamentally flawed service and individuals who go onto develop Chronic Fibromyalgia wouldn't simply be written off. You only need to be misfortunate enough to become ill to discover just how diabolically poor, unresponsive and uncooperative this industry really is. No matter which sector you seek help from, be it either the public or the private sectors, the service is abominable. No matter whom you consult or what level that representative may be, it doesn't matter what tests you participate in or what sort of investigation you undergo. These people know very little about very little and what they do know or articulate freely to you is generally outdated, self protectionist and complete and utter rubbish with no humanistic element to it. You see:

- How can it be that we still have a sociologically biased industry that is controlled from within?

- How can it be that we still have a sociologically biased industry that protects and rewards underperformance from those who support it or are employed by it?

- How can it be that we still have a sociologically biased industry that is afraid to acknowledge advancement in thinking until that change in approach is decades old?

- How can it be that we still have a sociologically biased industry where those who are employed in it have no idea about the majority of diseases and conditions they encounter?

- How can it be that every unexplainable condition can be written off by those within this industry as simply being of a psychological origin?

- How can it be that they're programmed as a service provider within this industry not to hear, help or support suffering and pain?

- How can it be that no matter what your own personal or professional credentials are, as soon as you engage with this industry you're immediately considered an intellectual cretin by those providing basic services within?

- How can it be that if you dare to challenge this industry from within you're immediately risking your career?

- How can it be that fighting for resolution from chronic illness can expose you to the pressure of clinical services being withdrawn from you?

And yet they all assume the same grotesque air of arrogance about who they are and what they are and how complicated your particular situation may or may not be. This bullshit they offload is by default, simply an outdated facade designed for a bygone age when we the general public were considered as intellectually inferior to representation from this industry. But this misguided assumption still exists today to mask clear inadequacies, ignorance and fragile egos yet the reality is that it's probably more disrespectful to us now than it ever was because we're all much smarter than this industry gives us credit for. This crux of my irritation is that this industry and those who support it are an affront to everything that is both decent and good in our modern world. We don't expect or accept bullshit and ridicule from any other private sector or public service industry. So why do we accept this institutional miscon-duct from the clinical world?

Well, the truth is that we really don't think that we have any pow-er to change our situation and at the point we commence any social intercourse with this industry we're already in a state of vulnerability and low vitality. Therein resides the reason why so many people with undi-agnosed disease states go onto to develop Chronic Fibromyalgia before ultimately being written off as a neurotic or a depressive with no possible chance of making an effective recovery. You see the medical/clinical industry is very adept at falsely blaming the symptoms of chronic disease states and ultimately Chronic Fibromyalgia upon the fragile psychology of any mortal who presents with such appalling and life debilitating conditions. But what is the truth behind this predisposition of our psy-chology being the root cause of all our chronic illness and chronic illness expression?

Well I'm going to look at that very point in the next chapter so please fasten your seat belt, but first check out the clinical abuse loop.

I live every day to the full now since I began to live again pain free

Surviving The Ignorant Clinical Abuse Loop

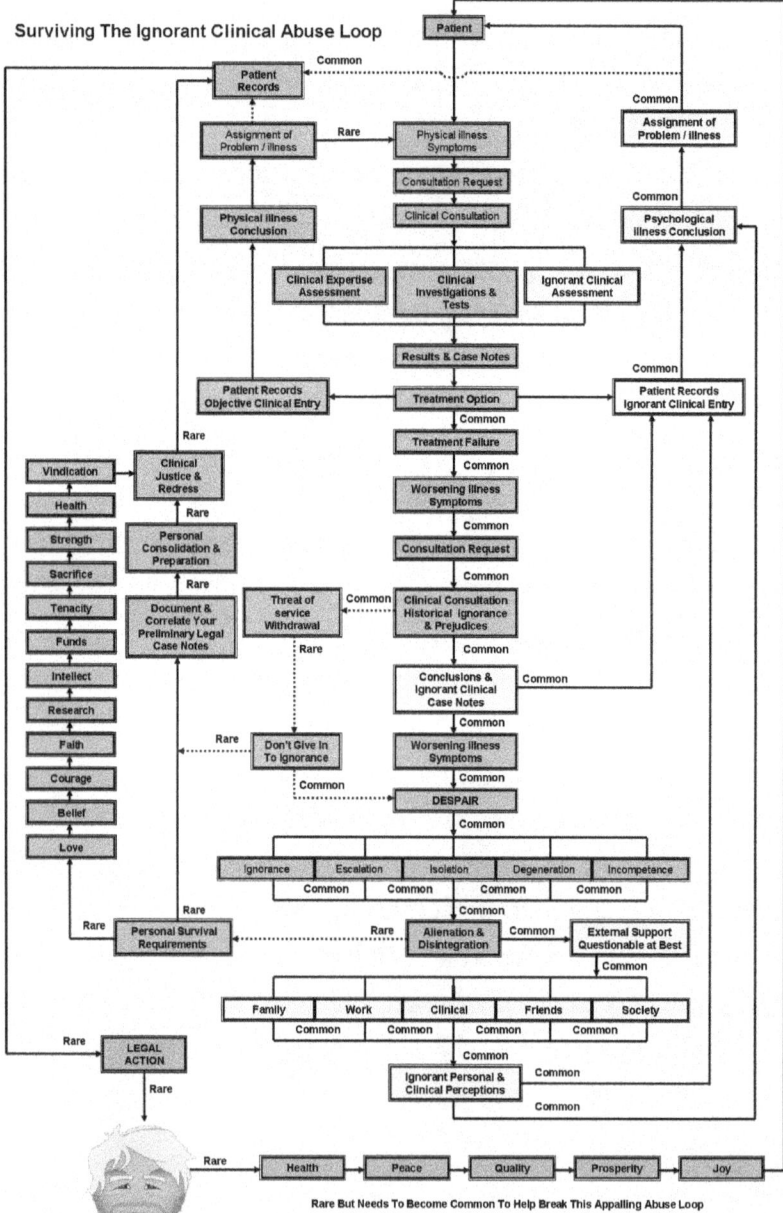

Patient

Patient Records — Common

Assignment of Problem / illness — Rare — Physical illness Symptoms

Assignment of Problem / illness — Common

Consultation Request

Physical illness Conclusion

Clinical Consultation

Psychological illness Conclusion — Common

Clinical Expertise Assessment | Clinical Investigations & Tests | Ignorant Clinical Assessment

Results & Case Notes

Patient Records Objective Clinical Entry | Treatment Option | Patient Records Ignorant Clinical Entry — Common

Rare

Treatment Failure — Common

Vindication | Clinical Justice & Redress — Rare | Worsening illness Symptoms — Common

Health | Rare

Strength | Personal Consolidation & Preparation | Consultation Request — Common

Sacrifice | Rare

Tenacity | Document & Correlate Your Preliminary Legal Case Notes | Threat of service Withdrawal — Common — Clinical Consultation Historical ignorance & Prejudices — Common

Funds | Rare

Intellect | Conclusions & Ignorant Clinical Case Notes — Common

Research | Common

Faith | Rare — Don't Give In To Ignorance | Worsening illness Symptoms — Common

Courage | Common

Belief | DESPAIR — Common

Love

Ignorance | Escalation | Isolation | Degeneration | Incompetence
Common | Common | Common | Common

Common

Rare | Personal Survival Requirements | Rare — Alienation & Disintegration — Common — External Support Questionable at Best — Common

Rare

Family | Work | Clinical | Friends | Society
Common | Common | Common | Common

Common

Rare | LEGAL ACTION | Ignorant Personal & Clinical Perceptions — Common

Rare | Common

Rare — Health → Peace → Quality → Prosperity → Joy

Rare But Needs To Become Common To Help Break This Appalling Abuse Loop

Battle For Life & Your Rights

At the point I began to understand my pain I knew my life had changed

EXPLORING PSYCHOLOGICAL ILLNESS PRAGMATICALLY

Exploration Five

I live every day to the full now since I began to live again pain free

At the point I began to understand my pain I knew my life had changed

How frequent is it for patients' problems to be simply written off as nothing more than a deluded psychology? Well far more frequently than you may expect. You see, there is a prescriptive culture within the medical world which has a predisposition for looking to offload all the patients' problems back onto them. It's basically part of the overall clinical abuse model and its guiding principles are no more than:

- When in doubt just call your patients illness a psychological problem.

- When tests don't indicate a deviation from normal values, just call your patients' illnesses a psychological problem.

- When imaging doesn't show up any abnormalities just call your patients' illnesses a psychological problem.

- When you simply can't be bothered with your patients' perceived or preposterous symptoms just call their illness a psychological problem.

But what is the truth and just what part does our psychology play in the bigger scheme of things when it comes to our health? Well first we need to understand that whilst we may be familiar with the term 'psychological illness' few of us know that the modern day originator of this scientific field was 'Wilhelm Wundt' who established the first psychology lab in Leipzig, Germany. Believing at the time that *properly* trained individuals should be able to *accurately* identify the mental processes that accompanied an individual's feelings, sensations, and thoughts. The emphasis here is upon *properly trained* individuals accurately identifying the processes that underpin the emotional predisposition of individuals in any given psychological state.

Now the development of this science didn't happen by chance, mankind in all its societies has battled throughout its entire documented history with the thorny issue of mental illness and insanity. That's why we in the United Kingdom still have such draconian measures as the 'Mental Health Act' where citizens can be sectioned and detained under said act for extended periods if they pose either a danger to others or more often than not simply a danger to themselves. Now there is absolutely no doubt that some individuals are insane, we see that in the likes of Shipman, Stalin, Hitler and Saddam Hussein.

The problem is there have been no major advances since time began to delineate between organic insanity and biologically insults that have the propensity to inflict insanity upon mankind. So we still have no way of knowing who's insane and who's simply biologically ill. I'm advocating therefore that the golden psychological card which is so readily used to explain the unexplainable illness i.e. there is a significant psychological component to your illness, is simply a complete red herring in the majority of chronic illnesses.

At the point I began to understand my pain I knew my life had changed

Those inaccurate value judgments simply have no clinical grounding upon which to base the assumptions of a psychological condition upon save for some cursory presenting symptoms.

Now it's that point of clinical evidence that I wish firstly to focus upon. You see; if you present yourself to a medic suspecting that you have let's say; possibly hypothyroidism. The first thing they will do is:

(a) Poo poo and ridicule you.

And then

(b) Perhaps agree reluctantly to give you a thyroid test.

They will then rattle on about how they couldn't possibly give you a trial of low dose thyroid medication until your tests results come back and prove that you do indeed have an issue with your thyroid. Yet the same medical practitioner within 5 minutes of another consultation will conclude with NO clinical data that you are indeed suffering from a psychological condition and therein he or she will feel eminently comfortable to prescribe anyone of a line of toxic psychiatric substances. It seems to me incredulous in the 21st century, that some unqualified cretin can make such sweeping statements about the condition of someone's psychology. More so when we realise that we pay these rogues insane salaries for the little that they do. Affording them great status to comply with the values and defining principles of the Hippocratic Oath. But my question is; do they deliver greatness for the greatness we bestow upon them? Well they're certainly paid insane salaries and afforded great status but very few of them have ever actually signed up to any form of; Hippocratic Oath. Furthermore it's fair to suggest that many of them don't actually know what the original Oath actually says despite the fact that they frequently hide behind it.

I actually look at that point further in the chapter Hippocratic Oath Or Merely Hypocritical Froth focusing upon specifically all the medical illusions that we as a society are sold.

Nevertheless I'm going to labour my point here of psychological postulation over scientific rationale, by asking this:

- If I have an abscess inside my mouth accompanied by intolerable pain do I have an abscess and intolerable pain?

Or

- Do I have a psychological problem which is manifesting the symptoms of pain?

Well clearly it's the first bullet point not the latter unless that is you're employed in the medical world. You see, in the medical world seeing is not always believing whereas in the presence of no rationale, believing is always right. It is that preoccupation with self importance and unqualified value judgments that continues to blight our medical records and destroy our lives.

But what if I substitute abscess for undetectable anomaly generating misery and great pain that flawed tests and investigations are unable to detect. What do I have then?

- Do I have an undetectable anomaly which is causing misery and pain?

Or

- Do I have a deep seated psychological problem that is manifesting symptoms of misery and pain?

At the point I began to understand my pain I knew my life had changed

Well of course it's the latter in terms of medical rationale because; the very fact that my problem cannot be found means that it simply doesn't exist. It must therefore be a manifestation of my fragile psychology which requires no further input from them. Is it any wonder that I regard these rogues as the lowest form of life?

It's clearly apparent to me now that in bog standard, tricky or complex medical investigation situations we the patients are always to a greater extent perceived to be the responsible party for the clinical problem we're experiencing because as mere mortals we have such fragile psychologies. Surely though this situation is truly insane, how can this industry say on one hand that, unless their outdated investigation techniques are able to detect a problem then it simply doesn't exist whilst in the same breath assign clinical labels to patients with the shallowest to zero investigations of their case?

I do not argue or disagree with the fact that our psychology plays a very big part in the way we cope with, or handle our difficulties. But it is not the root cause of all mans hidden or seemingly translucent diseases and I therefore repudiate the waving of the psychological cause golden card by cretins within the medical industry.

If our psychology was the root cause of the majority of illnesses then we would be able to see for ourselves the advances in the treatment of psychological conditions over the past hundred years. Because the money we spend on this aspect of medical care via so called research and residential care etc, is simply insane. The reality to my primary postulation is quite stark and I say that because the medical industry is having a laugh. Nothing much has changed in the diagnosis and treatment of these conditions despite the oceans of scientific papers that have been written.

I live every day to the full now since I began to live again pain free

There have been no major breakthroughs in clinical analysis, qualification or treatments of psychological conditions save for commercially sponsored indoctrination and use of debatably successful drugs. Now if anyone who has been put on those drugs has improved, all I can say is good for you, but for the majority of us who didn't need them in our body to solve our health condition, then I would respectfully suggest that they are:

- Dangerous

Or

- Complete waste of bloody time.

Yet the medical world's view remains without any validity that all illness derives from an emotional or mental state and that physical illness if it cannot be pinpointed simply doesn't exist. But surely these are the views of yesterday's men, the sorts who questioned the validity of;

- The shape of the earth.

- The purpose of the sun.

- The make-up of the moon.

- The relevance of the stars

They are the views of men who dared not seek to discover if the world was flat or round and who shouted heresy if a man sort to postulated different thoughts or articulated and challenged perceived truths.

At the point I began to understand my pain I knew my life had changed

The very fact that this approach happens almost by default in clinical surgeries throughout the UK, simply validates my position that the medical world is seemingly still stuck in the dark ages, ignorant and despite its protestations, doesn't really care. Were they motor mechanics with the same approach to problems these people would be simply unemployable or even in jail e.g.

- 'I'm sorry Mr. Hardy but I couldn't find anything wrong with your car, but incidentally have you ever tried counselling, sometimes it really does help?'

Or what about this favourite one;

- 'Yes I hear what you say Mr. Hardy but that is just a sensation of knocking at the front of your car, I'm the expert here I can't find any signs of knocking so perhaps its more of a psychological issue than you think, how's your sex life by the way?'

Two months later the engine in my car implodes;

- 'Oh well these things just happen sometimes Mr. Hardy, I've checked your notes and it would appear that your tyres and exhaust were fine when you were last in here, now you're clearly agitated so I'm going to suggest that there seems more to this than just an engine in your car, do you think you need to see a psychiatrist?'

- 'Answer, no I don't think I should see a psychiatrist you bull shitting waste of space, I was in here not so long ago and I told you that there was something seriously wrong with my engine and all you did was check my bloody tyre pressure and exhaust mounting. Now I'm back here today with a damaged engine and I'm asking you this, are you a bloody mechanic mate or simply a mechanic on your great grandmothers side of your family because your technical and professional capabilities are shoddy to say the least?'

The thing is if this happened in real life we would be straight to trading standards but when it comes to the medical industry we're all very guilty of not being prepared to take those bastards on. The public at large would be shocked if they knew just how little psychological or psychiatric training non specialists in that field actually undergo before they're let loose on us.

I liken their understanding of psychological or psychiatry to that of the fat clever bastard who we've perhaps sat next to as lovers of football in the football stands all around our country. You know the one I mean. From beginning to end he hurls his abuse and yet he's probably never played the beautiful game. Yet he's somehow deluded himself into thinking that he's some kind of football guru.

Well, the truth is that the average medic you will ever encounter has little to no training in either psychological or matters of psychiatry and as such are the least qualified of clinicians to prescribe conditions of that nature to you or about you. Yet they have bought into ignorant schools of thought which date way back to the 1920's.

At the point I began to understand my pain I knew my life had changed

Outdated schools of thought that postulated that we, as individuals, are responsible for all our own thoughts and our perceptions on life and that we all have demons and un-reconciled issues deep within us that frequently manifest themselves as illness. Today that belief is still perpetuated by our ignorant medics as a way of offloading the cause of a tricky problem back onto the shoulders of its originator simply because they know that they can do that.

So much so that you can bet your last £10 that if you encounter any extended or unexplainable medical issue at any point in your life, that the psychological postulations or dogma that will be rolled out or recorded on your medical records will be a derivative of some unqualified cretins understanding of:

- Personality Psychology – This specialist area looks at the various elements that make up individual personalities and includes Freud's structural model of personality as an example of a protagonist of this field.

However at the point a qualified psychologist is brought onto your case I can guarantee you that Personality Psychology which has already been used by medical ignoramuses as ammunition against you will be almost entirely dropped in favour of:

- Clinical Psychology Investigations – This specialty area is focused on the assessment, diagnosis, and treatment of mental disorders.

However the study of psychology has moved on tremendously since its conception and there are now many widely differing schools of thought and differing approaches to this challenging subject including:

- Cognitive Psychology - This specialist area is the study of human thought processes and cognitions, including topics such as attention, memory, perception, decision-making, problem solving, and language acquisition.

- Abnormal Psychology - This specialty area is focused on research and treatment of a variety of mental disorders and is linked to psychotherapy and clinical psychology.

- Social Psychology - This specialist area is a discipline that uses scientific methods to study social influence, social perception, and social interaction. Social psychology studies diverse subjects including group behaviour, social perception, leadership, nonverbal behaviour, conformity, aggression, and prejudice.

- Comparative Psychology - This specialist area is the branch of psychology concerned with the study of animal behaviour, believing that the study of animal behaviour can lead to a deeper and broader understanding of human psychology.

- Forensic Psychology - This specialist area is an applied field focused on using psychological research and principles in the legal and criminal justice system.

- Industrial-Organizational Psychology - This specialist area uses psychological research to enhance work performance, select employee, improve product design, and enhance usability.

- Developmental Psychology - This specialist area is the branch of psychology that looks at human growth and development over the lifespan. Theories often focus on the development of cognitive abilities, morality, social functioning, identity, and other life areas.

- School Psychology - This specialist area is the branch of psychology that works within the educational system to help children with emotional, social, and academic issues.

- Biological Psychology - This approach is the only area of accessible psychology that studies how biological processes influence the mind and behaviour.

Ironically though; Biological Psychology will never be rolled out unless you've been through surgery, a crash or a smash. Yet this approach is the only area of accessible psychology that studies how biological processes influence the mind and behaviour. Now there's no getting away from it *Biological Psychology* is still light years away from where it should be by now but at least it's sort of heading in the right direction. The only problem is as ever when undergoing medical interventions, your future will depend entirely upon the training of the psychologist responsible for driving any biological investigations. You may well find that in most instances he or she just simply reverts back to or refers you to another Clinical Psychologist on the grounds of costs or insufficient evidence to warrant extensive testing.

I live every day to the full now since I began to live again pain free

Throughout my darkest days I battled like a Spartan albeit a very ill Spartan to find the root cause of my illness and I was frequently told by medical representatives, 'no we're not testing you for this or for that'. Or 'we can't keep on testing for different things indefinitely Mr. Hardy you're simply going to have to understand that you have a psychiatric problem'.

Now there is absolutely no doubt that if we feel low it's difficult for us to feel happy until we shift our mind set. We see that day after day in the emotions and moods of ourselves and our kith and kin. It's simply preposterous to suggest to someone who is ill that if they change their mindset things somehow will resolve and they will feel better.

You see; life as we know is not like that, we are not like that, there are always impositions placed upon our bodies which make it impossible for us to feel happy simply as and when we choose to feel happy. The best we can ever hope to do is to recognise and accept that we have a part to play in that process yet understand that we do not always hold all the keys. So the question remains, is 'psychological illness real or simply a medical form of illness fiction?'

Well there's no doubt in my mind that there are many forms of psychological illness, but in the absence of firm biological data I cannot accept or agree that psychological illness is an illness in its own right. If the root course of a problem cannot be qualified then it MUST fall into the category of symptoms from an unknown disease. Therein there must be a concerted effort made to search out the origin of that disease and not simply to attempt to treat the symptoms with dangerous views, perceptions or drugs. Under no circumstance can an unknown disease be morally written off as an emotional or psychological illness because I would respectfully suggest that act in itself constitutes gross clinical malpractice.

At the point I began to understand my pain I knew my life had changed

I therefore advocate that anyone being written off by a medical representative, must document that incident via a formal communiqué to their practice in readiness for future legal action. It is only at the point we start bringing the medical industry to account, day after day that we will:

- Get the services we so desperately need.

And

- Weed out the 'luddites, rogues and charlatans' who shouldn't be in the industry in the first place.

The global market place we live and work in is full of medics desperately looking to explore new boundaries. So if we don't have the quality home grown medics that we need who are prepared to accept that we're all part of the 21st century. Then I say, lets simply offload the; 'luddites, rogues and charlatans' to the unemployed wastelands where they belong and lets import brighter, fresher service support professionals as we would do with plumbers, builders, electricians and engineers.

You see; as a former sufferer of all that's wrong with our insidiously flawed medical model we simply don't have the time, money or resolve to bring the luddite bastions of our medical industry kicking and screaming into line with our modern needs, standards and expectations.

We need effective medical services now, not light years from now, but tomorrow, or at the very latest the early part of next week. What's more we can all play our part in bringing about change; help create a medical model that is technically competent, robust and able to meet ALL our needs. Start today, and let's hope that no one ever has to document the level of personal suffering that I've been forced to document and voice via *Raphael's Legacy* etc.

At the point I began to understand my pain I knew my life had changed

EXPLORING LYMES DISEASE PRAGMATICALLY

Exploration Six

I live every day to the full now since I began to live again pain free

At the point I began to understand my pain I knew my life had changed

Be scared, be very scared if you live in the Scottish Highlands, the Lake District, the Yorkshire moors, the New Forest, The Welsh Hills, The Peak District, The Cotswold's, Dartmoor or any British town or village. For there is a disease so deadly out there it can literally destroy your life in a matter of days not weeks! But this disease is not one that you've probably ever been warned about; because this is a disease that our government and our chief medical officers refuse to accept is a major problem or even here amongst us today. So deadly is this disease that it can be spread through sex, through food, through the placenta, through ticks, through midges, through mosquitoes and through wild animals and domesticated pets that have fleas. The disease that I refer to is no other than the life sapping, body destroying, Lymes Disease or its official name the Borrelia burgdorferi Bb spirochete. Typical Lymes Disease symptoms include:

1. Sudden unexplained skin rashes with a whitish centre.
2. Joint pain.
3. Joint swelling.
4. Stiff neck.
5. Unexplainable fatigue.
6. Flu-like symptoms.

7. Frequent fevers and shivers.
8. Frequent sore throat.
9. Heart irregularities.
10. Depression & mood swings.
11. Digestion and stomach related problems.
12. Difficulty eating nausea or vomiting.
13. Muscle twitching or muscle cramps.
14. Indications of sinus infection.
15. Hypoglycemia.
16. Bell's palsy.
17. Carpal tunnel syndrome.
18. Vision problems.
19. No mobility in muscles or tendons.
20. Sensitivity to light and sound.
21. Cranial pain or symptom of pressure inside head.
22. Strange shivers up and down spine.
23. Dizziness unsteady on feet.
24. Seizures unexplained blackouts.

Typical Associated Neurological Problems include;

1. Manic–depression.
2. Short-term memory loss.
3. Poor concentration.
4. Slow mental processing.
5. Brain fog.
6. Sleep disturbances.
7. Hallucinations.

At the point I began to understand my pain I knew my life had changed

Lymes Disease the great pretender can also mimic;

1. Multiple sclerosis.
2. Anorexia nervosa.
3. Alzheimer's disease.
4. Parkinson's disease.
5. Bipolar depression & psychosis.
6. Hypothyroidism.
7. Fibromyalgia.
8. Guillain–Barré syndrome.
9. Cranial nerve disturbances.
10. Heart abnormalities.
11. Arthritis.
12. Gulf War syndrome.
13. Obsessive compulsive disorder (OCD).
14. Attention-deficit/hyperactivity disorder (ADHD).
15. Chronic fatigue and immune dysfunction syndrome (CFIDS).

Now I'm not going to dwell or delve too heavily into all the issues associated with Lymes Disease. But is important that we as a society sit up and tack notice of the fact that when we have a condition in our midst that is not responding to treatment, it is vitally important that we test patients for Lymes Disease. The reason being that I believe that bloody disease is wrecking too many lives is simply because its potential presence is not being considered or detected and instead people are just being fobbed off by clueless medics with diagnosis such as; ME, CFS, Depression, Stress, etc, etc, etc.

The difficulty however that we all face if we are infected with this disease is that there is a lot of misreporting about this disease, where common dictum suggests that:

(a) It doesn't exist in the UK.

And

(b) If you do contact it which is highly unlikely or so the medical world would say, it can be cured with a few short weeks of antibiotics.

Both those statements are completely wrong, it is here and you can be infected very easily and as yet there is no effective one stop or fully ratified treatment process through to cure.

On top of that diagnosing Lymes Disease can be a very difficult task, which is why so many cases are missed, or patients are diagnosed with other illnesses entirely.

You will acquire no support from the NHS in your endeavours to be either tested or treated for this disease and so it's very important to note that if you believe you have this condition you must take the initiative and privately fund your own investigations.

However please note that whilst there are a number of laboratories used to try to detect Lyme Disease the vast majority are notoriously inaccurate, often producing "false negative" results, i.e. showing that a patient does not have Lyme Disease when in fact they do and I can certainly relate to that.

Way back in 1988 I tried to engage my GP with the spectre of Lymes and was immediately poo poo'd by him. So I went out and had the wrong lymes test performed privately *which cost me a lot of money at the time* and it came back negative. The very fact that it came back negatively threw my chances of recovery completely off line for a further 17years whereupon in desperation I had the correct form of the test performed resulting in the confirmation of ballistic levels of lymes.

So why are there so many false negatives? Well the reason for this is due to the fact that the Borrelia burgdorferi spirochete is so adept at evading both our immune cells and conventional bacterial detection methods. In laymen's terms it's just too darn difficult to be detected by the protection processes in our body and by normal clinical processes used to detect disease. Borrelia burgdorferi, does not have one single, static appearance or chemical signature, and is able to alter these in order to evade detection. In this way, Borrelia burgdorferi is therefore able to evade standard laboratory testing procedures and when you add the fact that there are over 250 known strains of Bb, it becomes obvious that this truly is one very elusive bacterium.

I live every day to the full now since I began to live again pain free

It is not uncommon therefore for a patient to be highly infected by Lymes Disease only to repeatedly produce negative lab test results. You can see how these poor souls just like I was; get tarnished and written off by the medical world as neurotic and hence offloaded to the shit which is psychological and psychiatric intervention treatment regimes and zero treatment options designed specifically to address any underlying diseased states e.g. Lymes Disease. So then how are you going to make sure that if you have Bb that you:

(a) Identify it correctly?

And

(b) You identify it with the degree of speed you need?

Because

(c) It's important to note that every week wasted can add literally months onto the painful task of clearing this dreadful disease from your body.

Well you're going to have to either engage your clinical practice in the first instance or find some qualified person who can extract blood from you. You're then going have to contact the Bowen Research & Training Institute in North America and request their Bowen Q-RiBb test vials and transfer packaging etc. The term Q-RiBb stands for, Quantitative Rapid Identification of Borrelia Burgdorferi which is a relatively new test was developed by Jo Anne Whitaker, M.D. an international medical researcher and a Lymes disease patient herself. The method uses a fluorescent antibody technique on whole blood. As it is 'quantative' the test can determine the extent of infection and that is precisely why I chose the test for myself. A preliminary report of the findings is provided to the patient within 24 hours of receiving their blood specimen and final report including digital photographs is issued a few days later. Now that's what I believe medical investigations should be all about i.e. rapid testing and rapid reporting coming together as one. The other great thing about this test is that the Q-RiBb is the only test that is unaffected by whether the patient is currently or recently has been taking antibiotics. The reason that is important is because as previously mentioned Bb can detect when it's under threat and can change its form or identity via masking hence evading all other screening processes. It cannot evade however this screening method, so if you do have lymes this test will prove it.

Let's take this situation one step further now, let's assume that you have had your results and you have tested negative for lymes via Q-RiBb, what do you do? Well you do all that you can do to find out what's really wrong with you because that's all anyone of us can ever do. Assuming that you agree with me that laying down and doing nothing is simply no way to live or be. You see I personally dislike names and handles that are thrown out and anchored onto patients by the medical industry e.g. she has OCD, he has ME, she has MS, he has IBS, he has Lymes Disease etc. There is far too much of this and not enough help for patients with these terrible conditions. The unfortunate truth however is that we can either choose to live with those handles and use then as our crutch or we can battle and fight for a better quality of life. In the greater schemes of things it doesn't matter which sits most comfortably with us because as individuals in our own right we each have the right to choose which path we'll follow in life and it really is as simple as that.

I live every day to the full now since I began to live again pain free

Now if your tests are negative and you still choose to battle for a better quality of life then there is a stark reality that you're going to have to wise up to. You're never going to get the sort of help and support that you need from our fundamentally flawed NHS. I know its annoying that a terrorist bomber can get a blood transfusion to save his or her life and that a paedophile can have his coronary bypass performed regardless of the former suffering he's caused during his life. But that is the way of things and I know that it simply doesn't make sense that those 'deviants' can get what they want when they need it and yet no one either hears the suffering or pain of those amongst us infected with Lymes Disease. But that is precisely why we need detach completely from the hypocrisy of those who cite the Hippocratic Oath in order to moralize the actions they take.

By accepting and not allowing ourselves to get hung up on the way things truly are we actually empower ourselves. With that shift in perceptions we're able to accept that the NHS always fails the chronically ill and because of that we can never be let down by it ever again. It is only at the point that we begin to recover that we can begin to kick and scream out loud that our so called glorious NHS is nothing but a cash hungry dinosaur filled with brains the size of peas. But don't despair there is help out there and there are solutions to insurmountable problems to be found. All we need to do is be careful yet willing to explore the potential of alternative views on disease, the treatment of disease and our perception of living and life.

At the point I began to understand my pain I knew my life had changed

As a working class lad who fought tooth and nail for the NHS I never ever would have thought I would find my self saying that money is the only thing in clinical care that can move you out of the darkness and into the light. But if you are ill and wish to recover, I'm saying it loud and clear right now, you will need to read, to spend your own money and then spend and read some more.

There are no magic wands, no miracles or benevolent healers at hand; chronic illness recovery starts only when a proper diagnosis has been made and an effective treatment process undertaken. At that point and that point only can your unnecessary suffering start moving towards an end.

Nevertheless I always say this to anyone suffering from a chronic illness if you're not making any progress on the treatment regime that you're on, you've either had the wrong diagnosis or your treatment protocol is wrong. The only reason I can say that is because as you will read in the later chapter The Treatment Explorer, I've got a wardrobe full of treatment failure t-shirts.

However I'm not the sort of guy who will stick with a treatment if I feel it's false or an untruth; because my fervent belief is that for a return to health there must be a point when we finally get over the chronically ill pain and suffering hump. And if that isn't happening then the treatment isn't working and it's time to understand:

- Why not.

And

- What you need to do to move that situation on.

There are many diseases out there responsible for chronic illness, some apparently treatable some not, all I can say is if I'd bought into the rubbish that I'd been sold for years, I wouldn't be writing this book now because I would never have made any form of recovery.

Nevertheless I've covered a Bb test result coming back negative, but what happens when it comes back positive. Well sadly it's not much different from above, you won't get the sort of help you need from the NHS. You're going to have to:

- Apply a multi pronged approach to ridding your body of as much of it as you can, including the neurotoxin load that it has produced.

- You're going to have to get you endocrine system working well again as well as your liver to ensure that you're able to remove the remnants of this disease from your body.

- Above all you're going to have to be strong, because the journey through to recovery is both difficult and possibly lifelong.

At the point I began to understand my pain I knew my life had changed

Exploring the thyroid link pragmatically

Exploration Seven

At the point I began to understand my pain I knew my life had changed

During the early part of this millennium when my body and world were falling apart and I was being clinically abused on a daily basis, I spent tens of thousands of hours on the web searching for clues. I simply couldn't get my head around why there was so much ignorance, incompetence and reticence within the medical world to help me. It was like I was trapped in a sick horrible film, being forced to go round the same loop day after day. This was not a 'Bill Murray *Groundhog Day*' situation though, because that film's story line was all about acceptance, release, renewal and love. My groundhog days were all about abandonment, abuse, ignorance, it was a time of great learning, of great despair and a time of no rewards for a lot of personal courage and effort. Day after day I desperately tried to unravel the sheer misery of my condition, I did the spiritual cleansing and psychotherapy on one level yet I still believed that there must be a physical answer somewhere out there on another level.

I live every day to the full now since I began to live again pain free

I researched and researched with absolutely no support from any one and found to my horror many times that the internet is at best fast food intellect and at worse fast food salmonella. There is so much information on the web, but not all that information originates from good hearts, *I will leave that point there for now because I pick it up again later in my look at the internet.* All I will say is, don't believe everything you read on the web, because some of it is certainly from fraudulent sources.

Anyway, some of my linear, lateral and abstract symptomology searches sort of arrived at a possible crossover i.e. the butterfly connection or the possibility that I had Hypothyroidism.

This is where I must raise a very important point. As a society we're brought up to think that the cause of illness has one point and one point only and at the point we discover that causal point then we are able medicate and to make a full recovery. So when we see, hear or read about someone making a successful recovery from a condition and their condition sort of replicates the symptomology we're experiencing we automatically think wooo hooo, I have the answer!

Wrong, wrong, wrong, wrong, wrong, that model works well with bog standard conditions such as influenzas where symptomology can be effectively treated, but it does not work at all well with complex bodily breakdown issues presenting as illness. The reason I say that is because during the course of chronic illness a whole range of related and non related biological processes and systems may have been adversely affected or damaged. Those systems and processes by necessity must also be supported, nurtured and somehow given a kick start to enable whole body health. There is also the real possibility that the symptomology you're attempting to treat is nothing more than a higher or lower level presentation generated by a hitherto undiscovered state of disease in your body.

At the point I began to understand my pain I knew my life had changed

The reason I've sort of laboured that point is because when I was at a very low point in my life, I like so many people, read Diane Holmes book 'Tears Behind Closed Doors'. The book is an autobiographical and moving account of the medical ignorance she endured with undiagnosed Hypothyroidism. Similarly, the book also has a tenacious campaigning and informing theme, in support of the recognition of people suffering from this condition.

The combination of this passionate presentation on life, pain, love, research and championing for a cause, rightly generates an under-standable cult status and following in some circles for both the book and its author Diane Holmes. Now I've never met Diane, although I was fortunate enough to speak to her one day on the phone and she did seem to be a lovely compassionate lady. I have to say though that whilst her book is extremely informing, its weakness in my opinion is the fact that it has the propensity to generate almost obsessive belief in one single cause of illness i.e. the thyroid. That from my own personal experiences at the time I explored the thyroid connection is almost dangerous. I must state here that my previous statement is not to imply that either Diane or the theme of her book are postulating dangerous lines of approach for she merely states the obvious including; the absurdity, pomposity and igno-rance of the clinical world time after time.

Nevertheless, the simple fact of the matter is that we all love a great success over adversity story and Diane Holmes' recovery was simply all that and more. She certainly suffered but through adversity and belief she some how managed not only to make a remarkable recov-ery but to also document her story and then go on to campaign for greater awareness and support of her condition.

I live every day to the full now since I began to live again pain free

Never forget however that 'Tears Behind Closed Doors' was Diane Holmes' story and not yours, it is not a manuscript for wellness, it provides like many books *my own included* simple milestones and pointers along the way to your own unique recovery. You see if only all of us who had been chronically ill were able to recover fully and quickly through a single point diagnosis, then life would be so blissful. Life is not blissful though and because life is not blissful it's imperative that we as a society are not lured into thinking that we can repair our bodies using the same single point diagnosis formula that worked for someone else.

You see; I've been one of the unfortunates trying to recover my health thinking that because my body was indicating issues pertaining to hypothyroidism etc, which at long last I'd had found the answer to my prayers. After months of treatment my condition didn't recover and because of that I don't want anyone else to ever feel the level of despair that I felt when incorrect treatment after treatment did not improve my health.

Unlike Diane Holmes, I was never blessed with unequivocal bodily reassurance that my health issue had been solved. That's why I believe that when we are chronically ill we must explore every avenue and all possibilities. In essence we must rule nothing out and pencil everything in. Equally we must be able to understand when something is either working or not. If it's working then great, and if it's not, then its time to explore your condition and test for root causes again.

At the point I began to understand my pain I knew my life had changed

I was fortunate that I read 'Tears Behind Closed Doors' and I recommend that book to anyone concerned about thyroid conditions. I was also fortunate that I met Dr Gordon Skinner and Dr Barry Durant Peatfield personally during the time I was exploring hypothyroidism and hypoadrenalism. Because both guys' provided great care, humour and generosity, but more than that they were simply forward thinking clinical pioneers, not afraid to rock all the populist bull shitter's clinical boats. And whilst neither of those guys directly helped me to solve my problem they did nevertheless help me to understand the bigger picture of chronic health matter.

One of the best books I've ever read on this subject is by Dr Skinner and it's the (Diagnosis and Management of Hypothyroidism) published through (Louise Lorne publications, 22 Alecester Road, Birmingham B13 8BE). To meet Dr Skinner was a treat, to read his book even years later is to connect with his wicked sense of humour, his great fun for life, people and of course golf and football. Both he and Dr Peatfield will remain forever in my memories as gentlemen of the highest order without any shadow of a doubt. Both champions of conceptual health management, both catalysts in the development of my own holistic approach to health i.e. 'read the signs, remove your prejudices and explore the potentials before you, for no man has all the answers, but he may know a man who holds a few'.

Anyway, back to the theme of this chapter our thyroid role in illness. So what is hypothyroidism? Well it's a very serious condition that debilitates life greatly and can even kill if not picked up in time. Hypothyroidism means that the thyroid gland does not make enough thyroxine, a clinical presentation of which is often referred to as an underactive thyroid. This presenting condition causes many of our body's functions to either slow down or stop completely.

In contrast, if you have hyperthyroidism, you make too much Thyroxine and that presenting condition causes many of our body's functions to speed up.

What are the symptoms of hypothyroidism then? Well basically because all our bodily process systems rely to some extent upon the supply of thyroxine, when it's not made available in sufficient quantities every process and system in our body begins to 'slow down' and the symptoms that commonly occur include:

- Tiredness.

- Weight gain or loss.

- Constipation.

- Aches, pains in every part of body.

- Feeling cold.

- Dry skin.

- Lifeless hair.

- Fluid retention.

- Mental slowing.

- Depression.

- Mood swings and anxiety.

At the point I began to understand my pain I knew my life had changed

Less common symptoms include:

- A hoarse voice.

- Irregular or heavy menstrual periods in women.

- Infertility.

- Loss of sex drive.

- Carpal tunnel syndrome.

- Memory loss.

- Confusion.

- Dementia in the elderly.

Now all these symptoms can be caused by other conditions however, and so sometimes the diagnosis of hypothyroidism is not as straightforward as one may think. Symptoms usually develop slowly over time and gradually become worse over months or years as the level of thyroxine in the body steadily falls. It's understandable therefore that hypothyroidism can often be missed by the medical world whilst paradoxically often being seen as the root cause of so many diseased states by the chattering health concerned masses.

However as bad as suffering from undiagnosed hypothyroidism is, I believe you must consider yourself extremely lucky if you're able to recover from being chronically ill if you; place all your clinical intervention hopes at the door of one clinical interventionist theme. If you suspect your thyroid is becoming sluggish or hyper, it's important to find out why before you start medicating. Because if it's your adrenals that are the actual problem then you might just find that you end up in a significantly worse state of health than the one you're trying to eradicate.

Similarly, if you have some form of biological imposition that's impeding your body systems from working as they would choose to do so, then simply treating the higher level symptoms may achieve nothing more than aid in the propagation of a condition, when in reality you need to get on top of and hopefully remove.

My fervent belief is that only when your root cause analysis has been fully bottomed out and you're able to both instigate and validate the effectiveness of a treatment approach are you truly on the path to a better quality of life.

At the point I began to understand my pain I knew my life had changed

Now I'm not simply saying test, qualify and determine what's wrong with you just for the sheer hell of it. I know only too well that when we're suffering all we want is to get over the hump and get back to some form of meaningful life.

But I've encountered far too many people who are prepared to accept handles like, CFS, ME and Hypothyroidism who actually don't get well at all. Simply because they are not addressing the root cause of their problem, which in some instances can originate from multiple conditions.

Now I'm not a hard man with insensitive or overtly dogmatic views, I'm merely a pragmatist and a sufferer who's been through far too many mills. However I realise now at my ripe old age that only if we are prepared to put the work in ourselves, can we ever hope to reap our just rewards.

You see, any so called expert I put my faith in can say I have many things wrong with me. But if he or she can't treat me or make me feel better I'm not really interested in any rubbish they have to say.

Because at the end of the day their words are as empty as my life is without: wellness, happiness, peace and love. Therefore we owe it to ourselves to connect with our bodies when we're chronically ill, and only when our body informs us that we're making a healthy recovery should we accept despite our cross over symptoms that our diagnosis is right.

So whilst it's true that the starting point of every journey begins with the first step, I would nevertheless urge anyone suffering from a chronic illness condition to take that first step carefully. To compile as much information as they can before taking that first step and under no circumstance simply accept a treatment protocol on the basis that it sounds plausible or has worked for a hero or maybe a close friend of yours.

I live every day to the full now since I began to live again pain free

The return to optimum health is a process or evolution in the midst of iteration. Rule nothing out and pencil everything in, test, qualify and if the treatments not working then stop what you're doing and rethink your situation over again. The optimum health process map on the next page has been created to guide you through that process, so please connect with it and your desires for a better quality, because there's nothing complicated about having optimum health save for the chronically ill require it errrrrrrrrr.............right now.

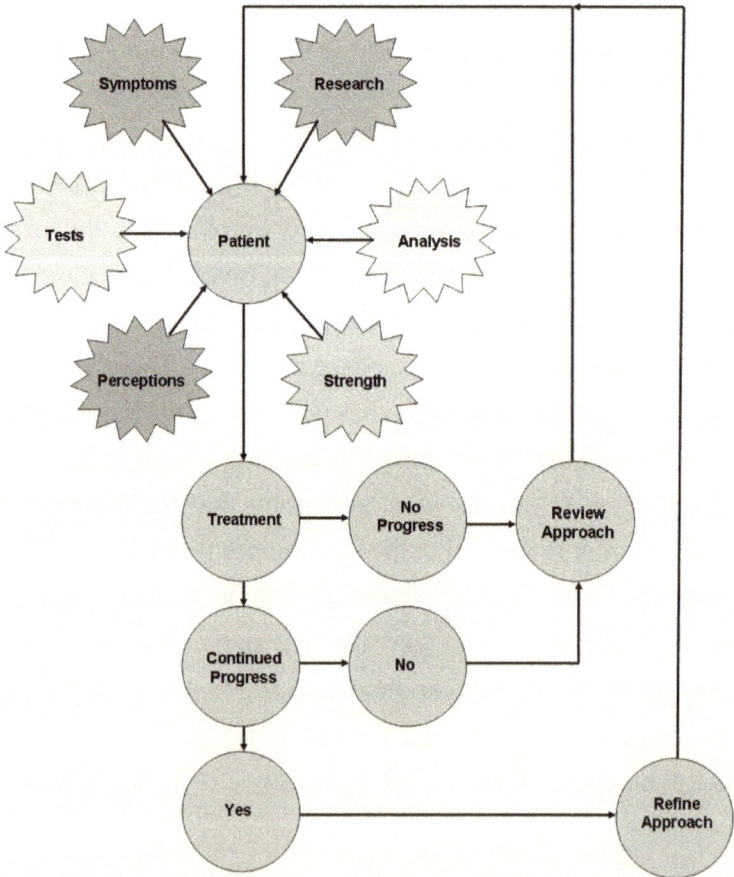

The return of optimum health, requires nothing more than optimum clarity of intent

At the point I began to understand my pain I knew my life had changed

EXPLORING GENETIC TIME BOMB LINKS PRAGMATICALLY

Exploration Eight

I live every day to the full now since I began to live again pain free

At the point I began to understand my pain I knew my life had changed

Whilst I've explored conditions, perceptions and diseased states from a highly personalised view point and position in this book. I nevertheless believe that my pragmatic views originate from nothing more than an enquiring mind, stimulated by great personal suffering and learning. I have no great gifts to bring to the world, no great deeds to accomplish; save to try to acquire some grace and peace in this life for myself and to be brutally honest it really doesn't get any more complicated than that. You see; I personally don't believe, having suffered far too much that there is any great majesty in suffering. I believe as an evolved society we should have gotten through most of our unnecessary suffering by now. Yet if there is anything rewarding about chronic illness and suffering it is that we have time to revisit things that we once took for granted. In doing so, we afford ourselves the opportunity to explore our life and backgrounds from newer and more informed perspectives.

During the process towards my own personal recovery I looked at my mum, her background, her health conditions and the imposition that may have placed upon me. Not really what you would can an implicitly abstract case but certainly one that allowed me to shed more light upon her and the impact that genetics can have upon us all.

My mum I'm informed was an extremely vivacious yet devout Roman Catholic, who had a zest for life complemented with a strong moral undercurrent. She loved people, animals, the outdoors and her favourite rugby team Whitehaven RLFC. She would frequently cycle hundreds of miles with her friends when not at work and help her dad in the garden taking much of his manual work. In fact nothing was a problem to her until she was struck down by two major illnesses in very quick succession. At 15 she was struck down by rheumatic fever only to sort of recover before being knocked for six at 16 with scarlet fever. My granddad, over the years I knew him, would frequently in his broad west Cumbrian dialect state, '*duz thou no marra, thee mother our Nancy was niver sham lass efter she ed scarlet end rumatic fever*'. He was indeed right, because from that point on:

- She would get tearful over silly things.

- She frequently had low moods.

- She would get tired quickly.

- She could sleep for England.

- Her thought processes were often confused.

- She was always cold.

- She always had pains in her joints.

At the point I began to understand my pain I knew my life had changed

By the time I was born and after much stress and much heartache my mum was already being treated with antidepressants and she'd already been written off as a nutter by her own family and my dad's callous and intolerant extended family. I spent all my childhood years removing and emptying buckets of urine from my parents' bedroom as my mum refused to leave her bed. Making her meals etc, and many, many times simply battling with her in floods of tears as I tried my level best to prevent her from committing or attempting to commit suicide whilst:

- My brother watched TV downstairs.

- My sister was in bed.

And more importantly whilst

- My dad simply lost himself in his horse racing or 4 pints of beer in kells legion or the red lion pub.

Such a life, such personal experiences at a tender age can be difficult to reconcile as we mature and I guess that's why I began doing so much work on myself at a very early stage in my life. The thing is, its only now that I've been through what I've been through that I'm able to totally forgive myself for any anger I had towards my childhood as well as any anger I had towards my mum for the dreadful childhood we had. I can't excuse either my brother or my father for their reluctance to engage or even to attempt to help or support my mum, but in reality I don't feel that I need to, they made their choices, that's just the way they are. It is however clear to me now that my mum has suffered greatly from social and clinical prejudices for the majority of her life.

I live every day to the full now since I began to live again pain free

She's been through hell, medications, had electrodes placed on her head, injections, psychiatric incarcerations, operations and physical and emotional suffering beyond belief. But to her testament she's still with us in 2008, alive and kicking for all her might, a colossus in terms of those who have alienated her, insulated her and ridiculed her for a lifetime of undiagnosed suffering and pain.

It's only now that I understand that she never ever recovered from rheumatic or scarlet fever, that her body was constantly in a toxic state, that her detoxing capabilities and her ability to cope were as impoverished as her finances and her limited joys in life. It's actually very upsetting now to understand just what she was forced to endure and also very annoying that this should have been imposed upon my mum. All of her suffering and years of waste through nothing more than sheer medical ignorance and the sociological prejudices of her kith and kin.

Now the reason that I've covered my mum's predicament is because I believe that it's eminently possible that our health can be compromised at any time in our lives by a raft of unseen genetic time bombs. I refer of course to placenta transferred neurotoxins and low grade disease states; I refer to industrial chemicals and toxins trapped in our DNA. I refer to genetically damaged biological process systems and organs all of which constitute a variable and a ticking time bomb in our ultimate physiological state of wellbeing. Now the previous postulation is not as abstract, challenging or as ridiculous as it would first appear. You see in days of yore man discovered that if he planted his weakest fruits of the harvest, his harvest the following year was a disaster. However when he planted his finest fruits his harvest the year after that had vitality and there was food in abundance. In essence he was proving that vitality propagates vitality, whereas disease propagates deformity and living matter with a reduced vitality.

At the point I began to understand my pain I knew my life had changed

Well we as individuals in our own right are nothing more than the products of our parent's fruits, a product of their vitality or paradoxically a product of their diseased states and a myriad of other things. There has been some research on this matter specifically focusing upon the impact of holocaust experiences upon the lineage of survivors. But whilst results have concluded that biological systems have been impaired in the majority of instances, no global acceptance of hereditary impositions via such roots has been forthcoming as yet. A position I would suggest is more to do with medical prejudices and historical perceptions than it has to do with due consideration and clinical expressions of acceptable probabilities. But then again we know that the medical industry is the last remaining bastion of, antagonistic, for the sake of it and protectionist luddite men.

Unfortunately however, research into the imposition of historical toxic lifestyles, the industrial revolution, chemical warfare, chemical manufacturing and disease is negligible. Yet we know that all those variables killed our forefathers with impunity but not before their fruits were sown with other such contaminated souls in the creation of whole new generations. For instance, my modern industrial contamination lineage consists of coal mining, steel making, mustard gassing, textile manufacture, nuclear generation / reprocessing and chemical manufacture to name but a few. Now there is no way that you can convince me that the toxic cocktails that my family worked in, breathed in or were impregnated with before eventually killing them is not in some way playing a significant part in my life story. Simply because it's impossible for them not to be that's why I believe we need to stop simply living in the moment and start building smarter profiles when we become, because that's the only way we're ever going to get the full picture and put the stabbing in the dark approach to bed finally and for good.

I live every day to the full now since I began to live again pain free

We know so little about the complexities of DNA toxic transfers, but we know that excess exposure to radiation and many forms of toxins be that, poisoning in low or high dosage, does effect and can damage a host's DNA. We know this because people die from such impositions it's as simple as that. Our DNA is nothing more than a blueprint from its previous owners and if their DNA was damaged, why shouldn't ours be equally damaged and prone to very subtle levels of developmental, repair and replication discrepancies which manifest at any point in our lives as subtle disease states?

I will take that one stage further. What if subtle issues with our DNA don't actually present themselves as a disease state later in life? But actually contribute to new disease states simply because the impositions placed upon our bodily functions, due to impediments in our DNA, render them weaker or less able to deal with the issues they're presented with. What if 'Barry Hardy' was born with historical mitochondria conjugates, which meant that my body's ability to detox at a cellular level was significantly compromised prior to point zero? Why then shouldn't I go on to develop serious and chronic health conditions? No matter what my body tries to do to fight off disease invaders, it's simply unable to offload the by-products of that battle and therein my body becomes toxic.

I hope you see where I'm coming from here, we all must have encountered chesty friends at school, kids who's summers were a nightmare due to hay fever etc, but neither us or they truly knew the origins of such impositions. Equally until we ourselves are presented with a health challenge we naturally believe that we were born healthy and that we've just sort of picked up a disease later in life. But my point is, unless we explore all avenues, all reasonable lines of research we have no idea what sorts of ticking time bombs lay deep within us. Because of that we may never truly understand what it is that we really need to do to return us back to some form of quality of life once we've been struck down by a chronic illness.

I'm therefore advocating that lineage must be considered when exploring possible imposition sources to our health issues, but word of mouth and subjectivity in the detection process are simply not good enough.

We need to test and look for clues, for markers and for answers, because deep within us may just be the key that we've been looking for. That must be our starting point to recovery, the point we've prayed so hard for and I say that with all seriousness because I advocate that the legacy of more ignorant times may indeed still be wreaking havoc with the life forces trying to live in so called, more enlightened times.

To fully appreciate what I'm saying here we need to stop biologically living in the moment, we need to stop making snap shot biological value judgments, we need to accept and appreciate that we are the products of yesterday's men and women. We live in bodies that are nothing more than receptacles of historical DNA, the very same DNA that was malnourished and poisoned, generation, after generation, after generation. So the next time you get angry about the imposition your health places upon you, stop your thought process right there and take the time to connect with:

- Who you really are.

- What you really are.

And

I live every day to the full now since I began to live again pain free

- The suffering that your DNA experienced long before it manifested itself as you.

Simply because

- Your body may only be trying its best to deal with the fall-out imposed upon it by the historical damage imposed upon your historical DNA.

On a more personal note if there's any spark of delight I take from the formulation of this chapter it's that I realise and I'm fully content with the fact now that; with no birth children to my DNA my DNA and all that it is, is effectively over at the point I take my last breath.......yay.

Perhaps part of my battle to refine my Raphael Treatment Protocol (RTP) was nothing more than to arrive at that point, who knows, and furthermore, who save for me, really cares because in truth it was only my life path to walk anyway.

At the point I began to understand my pain I knew my life had changed

A Personal Closure

People often remark about the beauty of birth and then fail whole-sale for a whole host of reasons to rejoice daily in the beauty of any given substance of birth. Similarly those very same people seem compelled to shy away from for the absoluteness that is our mortal passing, feeling it inappropriate to either discuss or explore the very essence of mortality. I've never had those problems, for I've always endeavoured to rejoice in the beauty of all the products of birth and am blessed enough to see our mortal finality as nothing more than blessed release from the pain we've endured for so long.

There is absolutely no sadness for me when a souls time is finally up, for I simply thank it and them for all that he, she, they were and for all that he, she, they aspired to be. At that point there is something deep inside me that allows me to let him, her, and them go to the place where their energy at that point needs to go and/or be. So I've shed very few tears over a blessed departure from mortality during my life, for I know that they all spent their time amongst us well and for that I feel nothing but unquestionable pride and admiration of and for them including the major part they played in my life.

It's important to note here that whilst I do not and never will shy away from the rigors of mortality, I'm tormented by its love, its finality and the great loss that it inevitably brings to us all. My belief is that when we connect in mortality we certainly learn to grow, but after that growth spurt we are often left with far too much time to reflect and participate in self flagellation based upon highly preventable regrets. That is I suspect one of the many frailties that we all encounter in being simply a mortal, maybe that's a life challenge that we all as mortals need to accept or at least try to conquer, but when all said and done who amongst us truly knows?

At the point I began to understand my pain I knew my life had changed

EXPLORING TOXIC BODY SYNDROME

Exploration Nine

I live every day to the full now since I began to live again pain free

At the point I began to understand my pain I knew my life had changed

In pursuit of recovery from my chronic illnesses I was forced to look at illness from a completely different perspective to that which I was brain washed with as a child. Subsequently, my personal health struggles have proven to me:

(a) Just how insidiously corrupt that brain washing was.

And

(b) Just how appallingly ignorant our medics really are.

The simple fact of the matter is that:

(a) Few medics truly understand the dynamics of illness.

And

(b) Few are prepared to shift their perception of illness preferring instead to adhere to the medical clap trap they bought into as part of their so called medical training.

I live every day to the full now since I began to live again pain free

Because of that it's very difficult when we're chronically ill to get any form of logical or scientific input from the medical industry full stop. Patients are written off at best and blamed at worst when presenting themselves to a medic with anything more than a cold, stomach bug or pain in the chest. It's like medics simply don't get illness at all, it's like illness is a great mystery to them which I struggle to comprehend really.

They don't seem to understand cause and effect, they don't seem to understand variable input dynamics and they don't understand basic physiology over and above basic anatomical understanding. In essence I've simply never come across an industry with such high levels of occupational ignorance towards the service it provides and for me that truly marks that industry as antediluvian *(old fashioned)* and as such no longer worthy of my respect.

Therefore when we are faced with chronic illness it's imperative that we take full ownership of our problem because it is the only sure fire way of making any progress. You see, chronic illness has many genera-tors and we must understand that dynamic if we are to ever fully recover. Happily the majority of what we need to know as laymen in terms of illness is not rocket science either; its just common sense, body monitor-ing and holistic treatment management.

Now it may sound astonishing but it is eminently possible that the vast majority of chronic illness perpetuation and relapse results from nothing more grandiose than toxic body syndrome *TBS*. Now I can just hear the howls of derision from the medical world, *'You joker Hardy I've never heard such tosh; toxic body syndrome, away with you man you're talking through your arse'*. Well before you the non medical readers of this book all jump the gun too, just hang on before you too commit to that assessment to

At the point I began to understand my pain I knew my life had changed

You see, were I a medic I might be able to talk through my arse, but I'm not; I'm like you a former sufferer of chronic disease, therefore if you will bear with me I will explain TBS as a pragmatist and man of engineering science. TBS is a state of bodily function that prohibits optimum health because the regenerative processes and capabilities of the body are in a constant state of compromise. The very fact that a body is so compromised moves that body into a toxic bodily state, are you okay with that. You see; at the point we move into a toxic body state our expressions of disease always presents with 5 main features i.e.

1. Mood Swings.

2. Fatigue.

3. Pain.

4. Anxiety.

5. Depression.

Talk, live or read about anyone with a long term chronic illness and the key presenting features of that condition will be the above and it is that phenomenon that I'm now suggesting are predictable derivatives of TBS. The reason they are predictable is because they are classic expressions of disease resulting from the deviation of normal values of hormones, neurotoxins, funguses, viruses and bacteria within any given bodily state.

You see; when any irresolvable imposition is placed upon our body, it quickly moves into a toxic state due to the break down in our methylation and sulphanation processes and as such the classic and consistent expression of that toxic state are; Mood Swings, Fatigue, Pain, Anxiety and Depression.

I live every day to the full now since I began to live again pain free

Now talk to a medic about TBS and he or she will simply poo poo it because:

(a) They are occupationally ignorant to disease generators.

And

(b) We are still light years away from having mainstream tests and/or a medical culture etc., in place capable of looking at illness with any degree of scientific clarity.

But the reality is; at the point we as individuals begin to look at our own illness with a degree of personal clarity we begin to understand what it is we must do to aid our recovery. What I'm suggesting here is that the linear progression of chronic illness through the standard hierarchy expression of; Mood Swings, Fatigue, Pain, Anxiety and Depression is nothing more than an expression of TBS. The key to understanding TBS is to accept that it is not bacteria, micro-organisms, viral infections and fungal infections that are the greatest impediments to optimum health. It is the derivatives of those impediments in the form of neuro and bio toxins that are the greatest long term hindrance to optimum health and the intrinsically linked failure and/or underperformance of our methylation and sulphanation processes. You see it is the toxic derivatives of diseased states that;

(a) Saturate our body during disease.

And

(b) That we are unable to expel that create the TBS state.

At the point I began to understand my pain I knew my life had changed

When our body however is under constant assault from neuro and bio toxins we are indeed in a state of TBS there can be no scientific argument against that. The real difficult aspect of this suggestion however; is getting to grips with the reality that in both high and low circulating TBS levels; the hierarchy expression of; Mood Swings, Fatigue, Pain, Anxiety and depression remains constant.

You see, such is the potency and potential corruptibility of TBS that our bodies are thrown out of balance very easily. Because of that it may be difficult initially or certainly prior to corrective intervention to determine whether a body is in a high or low circulating state of TBS or is simply being compromised by a high or low overall TBS load. The reason for that is that the neuro and bio toxins that underpin TBS are stored deep in body fat including the brain and it is only at the point that we begin the process of toxin removal that we begin to understand our TBS load.

TBS loading by default is unique to each individual because it's eminently possible to experience TBS from high levels of circulating toxins whilst having a relatively low overall TBS loading. The reason for that is because some of us are extremely poor at storing toxins in our body or creating additional body fat to store toxins there-in. The paradox to that is that some of us are very good at storing toxins in our body and generating additional fat to store those toxins. So that whilst there may be low circulating TBS, the originator of that circulating load can in some instances be a very high overall TBS load.

I live every day to the full now since I began to live again pain free

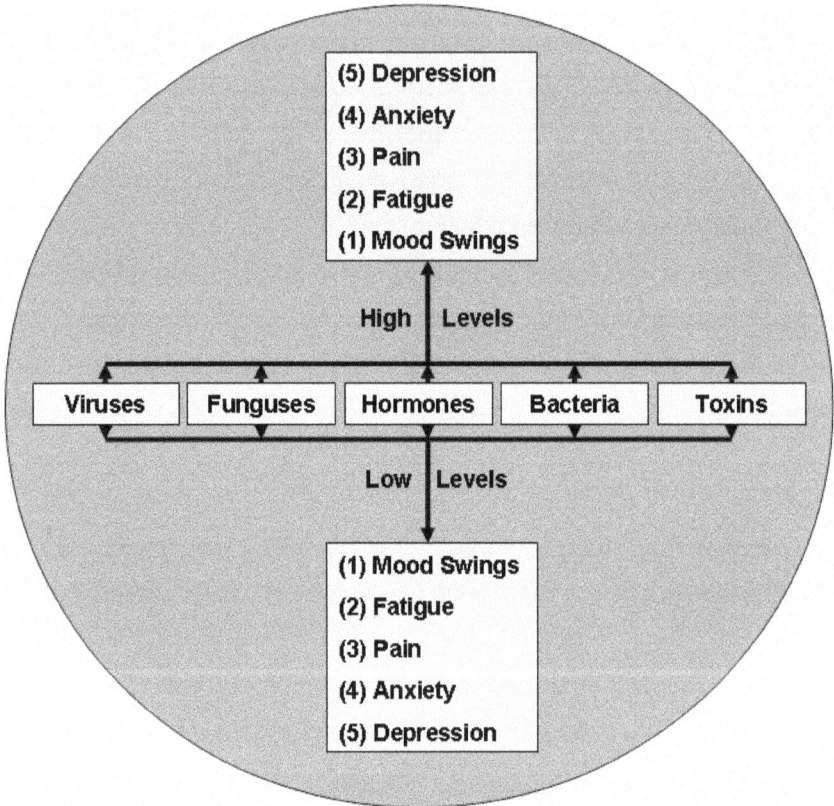

Toxic Body Syndrome

One of the main reasons that TBS is such a challenging condition is because:

(a) Its presence is counter to all our former belief structures in terms of illness definition.

And because

At the point I began to understand my pain I knew my life had changed

(b) TBS in the most part exhibits symptoms in the form of central nervous system expressions which sociologically are always regarded as being of a psychiatric origin.

In that situation all ill informed TBS sufferers immediately fall into the trap of self blame and self doubt about what's actually going wrong or on in their bodies. A situation compromised still further by the fact that any medic they consult in relation to their symtomology expression invariably re-assigns the blame for their condition back onto them. Where in reality the dynamic is very simple:

(a) Low overall diseased state and low toxin load results in a balanced body state re: fig 1 below.

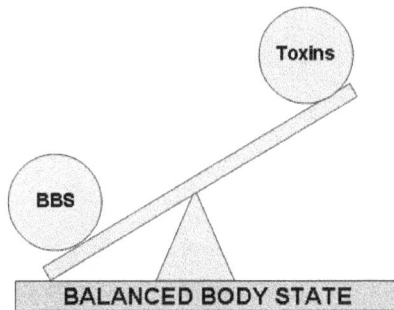

Whereas

(b) A high overall diseased state and high toxin load results in a toxic body state re: fig 2 below.

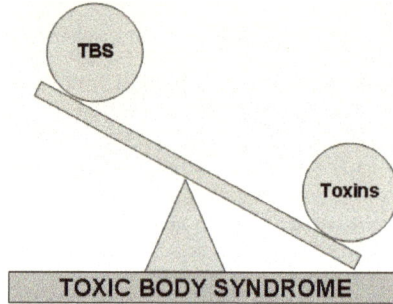

Now look I haven't just created a new acronym for the sake of it, the reason I'm bringing TBS to your attention is because actually its time that TBS was recognised. TBS is a chronic state of disease expression that is completely ignored by the medical industry and furthermore there is no effective mainstream or acceptable treatment option available to those suffering from TBS. Yet this state of bodily underperformance indiscriminately destroys lives and the quality of life and the real scary thing is that anyone of us can succumb to TBS at any point in our lives. Because whenever we move into a diseased state be that generated via a micro-organism, viral or fungal imposition and our sulphanation and methylation processes begin to falter. We potentially move into chronic TBS if our body is unable to deal or cope with the original imposition and/or its derivates e.g. toxin generation. The reason being that there is always potential for;

(a) Our cellular detox capabilities to stall completely.

(b) Our body's immune system to begin to deviate from norm.

And

(c) Our core TBS symptoms to cloud our actual clinical condition.

However be under no illusion that no matter what liver function analysis that you may have states; or how much detoxing you embark upon; TBS will be a present factor in chronic illness expression until the bodies overall TBS load is lowered or removed from the body completely. So then how do we initially test for TBS? Well you can't determine TBS via blood analysis you must undergo body fat biopsy and analysis, because that is where your TBS load resides. Okay; assuming that an excessive lipo-toxin load has been identified how do we lower it?

Well in truth and as yet I've not encountered a definitive protocol which eradicates this condition completely and believe me I've tried everything possible out there. However far infrared saunas certainly help to some degree and I'm sure that lipo-suction offers great potential, one of the areas of investigation however that I yet to personally undertake.

Nevertheless we all as individuals in our own right have to find a holistic range of techniques and protocols specifically designed to lower lipo-toxin loads which are not derivatives of ingestion detox and cleanse protocols. Because those are spectacularly unhelpful in terms of TBS eradication, simply because TBS is an insidious condition, dur to the fact it throws our entire body into a state of self destruct. When we're battling with TBS it can often feel as if everything we try to do to aid our recovery is continually disrupted by the influences of TBS.

I live every day to the full now since I began to live again pain free

So it's not by chance that chronically ill individuals like myself move from lean muscle mass into surplus body fat generation we suffering from TBS. You see; I'm now one of those individuals who's bodily detox capabilities are so flawed that the only way my body can cope with my TBS load is to generate greater levels of body fat to encapsulate it in. The harder I work to lower my TBS load, the more toxins I release from their fat rich tomb and harder my body works to generate superfluous body fat to re-encapsulate my toxins in. The down side of that is:

(a) An increased risk of lipo diseased states.

And

(b) Every time I burn fat I'm thrown once again into intolerable TBS diseased state expression.

Nevertheless it's not all doom and gloom, my personal research and subsequent self testing in terms of lowering my own TBS expression has enabled me to enhance my own quality of life and so I'm confident that I will discover the optimum formula for lowering TBS expression in due course. For anyone diagnosed or experiencing TBS I say only this:

(a) Accept that you have a highly toxic soup trapped deep inside you.

And

(b) Do all that you can possibly do to eradicate that from you body.

But

At the point I began to understand my pain I knew my life had changed

(c) Under no circumstance embark upon any radical detox or dieting campaign for there is real danger if you do of you imposing an increased health risk upon your already fragile health state.

The road to TBS recovery starts with acceptance of the condition, followed only by an educated and holistic approach to lowering its insidious disease expression. Because the key to ultimate progression in anyone's pursuit of well-being is to understand that it is a toxic body that creates a toxic mind, not a toxic mind that creates a toxic body.

However at the point toxins are removed from the body, the mind clears, hopes rise and fullness in life can once more be ours to enjoy free of all unnecessary pain.

At the point I began to understand my pain I knew my life had changed

EXPLORING ARTHRITIS PRAGMATICALLY

Exploration Ten

I live every day to the full now since I began to live again pain free

At the point I began to understand my pain I knew my life had changed

There is nothing funny about arthritis save for the comical way that people refer to the condition e.g. *'our GP says that jims got bloody arthurritious now so he's told him to lose some weight and start jogging'.* Oh yes you can bet your last £10 that at the point some ignorant medic decides that you've got arthritis, their next statements will be 'lose some weight' and 'take up some exercise'. But the ironic thing is that the flawed diagnosis of arthritis only really creeps into the diagnosis when we've a bit of age about us. Very few of us are ever tested for this condition unless for some unexplained reason, our body's immune system goes into freefall and general arthritic symptoms are the main presenting symptoms. So as an opener let me give you three classic instances of clinical dismissal for the same presenting symptom:

- Young athlete goes to his GP complaining about a terrible pain in his knee, GP says: 'hmmn, stop running and take these e.g. anti-inflammatory tablets' Young guy says, 'Sorry I can't take them I've got chronic gastritis and those will make my condition worse' GP says 'hmmn stop exercising and see how you get on' End of consultation.

- Young fat guy goes to see same GP complaining about a terrible pain in his knee, GP says: 'hmmn, you need to lose some weight and start taking more regular exercise'. Young guy says, 'Sorry I can't exercise man because I can hardly walk'. GP says, 'hmmn ok take these anti-inflammatory tablets for a month and see how you get on'. End of consultation.

- Middle aged guy goes to see same GP complaining about a terrible pain in his knee, GP says: 'hmmn, you need to lose some weight and start taking more regular exercise apart from that there's nothing I can do because you've got arthritis'. Guy says, 'Sorry I can't exercise man because I can hardly walk'. GP says, 'hmmn ok take these anti-inflammatory tablets for a month and see how you get on'. End of consultation.

Can you see the point I'm making? Do we really need to be paying our front line medics such outrageous salaries for that sort of non clinical appraisal? The thing is there is always an undercurrent of dogmatic, perceptions and a complete lack of empathy or desire to help the patient. A position compromised still further by the addition of secondary conditions or complications, via the only treatment option open i.e. stomach upset and/or further damage to the damaged knee through inappropriate exercise etc.

At the point I began to understand my pain I knew my life had changed

But what is Arthritis? Is it simply just pains in our joints or is there more to this condition than the majority of us realise? Well Arthritis is a chronic, progressive and disabling auto-immune disease affecting large sections of our population. It is an incredibly painful condition, can cause severe disability and ultimately affects a person's ability to carry out everyday tasks. The disease can progress very rapidly, causing swelling and damaging cartilage and bone around the joints. Any joint, muscle or tendon can be affected but it is commonly those physiological mechanisms directly related to hands, hips, shoulders, knees, feet and wrists that are at greatest risk. Furthermore Arthritis is a systemic, disease which means that it can affect the whole body and internal organs such as the lungs, heart and eyes. There are over 200 types of arthritis or musculoskeletal conditions, which are split into three classifications:

- Inflammatory arthritis such as rheumatoid arthritis, ankylosing spondylitis and gout.

- Non-inflammatory arthritis such as osteoarthritis, scoliosis and torn ligaments.

- Connective tissue disease such as lupus, sclerosis and Sjogren's syndrome.

Typical drugs used to treat arthritic conditions include;

- Cortisone.

- Ibuprofen.

- Indomethacin.

I live every day to the full now since I began to live again pain free

- Ketoprofen.

- Ketorolac.

- Mefenamic acid.

- Meloxicam.

All have differing success rates and all have associated side effects and potential complications, but none of them actually cure the disease. The best that they do is mask some of its main presenting symptoms, i.e. pain.

However it's only when you really start to examine this condition that you realise that the medical world, in terms of treatment and cure, simply hasn't got a clue. The industry rambles on endlessly about diet and exercise but seems resistant to any form of root cause analysis.

Time after time, international Arthritis research appears to show that whilst there are high instances of Arthritis in the developed world, in the undeveloped world the instances are quite low. But how can people in the undeveloped world be virtually free of this condition whilst we in the developed world appear to be tormented by this so called complex condition? Is it simply that we:

- Have the wrong diet?

- Don't get enough exercise?

- Simply a combination of the two?

- Or is there something still missing from the loop?

Well the picture is not as clear as it would first appear. This is because whilst there are clearly low instances of Arthritis in some areas of the undeveloped world. In other areas of the world where more ancient civilizations resided *which now forms part of our modernistic views of the developed world.* There is significant evidence to suggest that Arthritis was an endemic condition within those populations too.

You see, it has been discovered that amongst the indigenous population of North America, skeletons have been found dating back several thousand years which do show evidence of Arthritis. As a result of those findings there are some who have postulated that it is the presence of Arthritis in North America that potentially holds the key in terms of the manifestation of Arthritis in Europe. Citing perhaps some link to food groups, like potatoes and/or tobacco etc, for the manifestation of Arthritis in Europe that we now see.

But the only premise for that conclusion is that prior to the 1800's there was no detailed medical documentation of the condition in the British Isles or Europe. However, whilst the condition may not have been documented, we know from our own archeology that there is significant evidence to suggest high instances of cultural and non cultural Arthritis in the British Isles.

Therefore I simply don't believe the theory that indigenous foods from North America are responsible for the dispersal of Arthritis across Europe. I actually think it's all much simpler than that. I believe the problem is twofold, I believe it has both a gene pool DNA link accompanied by a genetic disease pool link. Both of which can be simply explained in the two points over the page:

1. Malnutrition can certainly have an impact upon the way our bodies develop and respond to disease over time and there's absolutely no doubt that the indigenous peoples of North America and Europe experienced starvation and famine, generation after generation. I'm therefore happy to postulate that the initial Arthritic gene pool link is that of malnutrition. A bodily condition which disrupts compromises and/or destroys at very subtle levels, every process and system in the human body right down to our very DNA expression. It's no wonder then that offspring from populations subject to frequent malnutrition exhibit subtle changes in their DNA including their ability to retain and assimilate vital vitamins, mineral and other key process growth and repair essentials.

2. If we then add an external diseased state like lets say: Lymes Disease in the case of North America and Syphilis in the case of Europe. We then clearly have all the components needed to generated high levels of inflammation and bodily breakdown. Because we know that the eradication of spirochete disease is extraordinarily difficult to achieve because the disease has the propensity to lay dormant for years upon years before being re-energized. So my question is, why wouldn't these diseases be playing a major part in Arthritic complaints, well I believe that the only barriers to that suggestion is anything more complicated than this; it's the depth of ignorance that exists within our implicitly amoral medical and clinical institutions.

At the point I began to understand my pain I knew my life had changed

But how insane is this postulation? Well not really that insane at all because, for thousands of years the people of North America and Europe have battled famine, Lymes and Syphilis Disease because it wasn't until the introduction of penicillin as recent as the 1940's that mankind started winning some of the battles that we have with vicious bacteria.

However guys like Samuel Hahnemann as far back in 1810 where postulating new ways of thinking on matters of disease, cause and transfer in order to move us away from the barbarism that was the medical world in those days, so my views today are really just a play on his words then. *Hahnemann believed that the cause of disease is the disturbance to our life force and that disturbances in that force manifest themselves as specific symptoms. The Law of Susceptibility deals with the invasion of the body by diseases referred to as Miasms. These Miasms can be acquired acutely or they can be congenital or latent, until some negative experience or normal aging triggers their appearance as a symptom and then as disease.*

It is both our historical genetic malnutrition and genetic low grade diseased states that I believe are the fuels that constitute the presentation of Arthritis in our societies right now. The absence of Arthritis I believe in other ethnicities is down to nothing more than the presence of antibacterial and antimicrobial foods in their diet.

Now I know what I'm postulating here can be a little challenging because whilst we can relate to historical famines etc, it's difficult for any of us to relate to another man's disease let alone an historical, diseased state. Nevertheless the fact of the that matter is that both Lymes Disease and Syphilis are spirochete bacteria, both of which bring about a whole host of inflammatory conditions including degradation of cartilage, muscles and bone through systemic neurodegenerative processes. Both Lymes Disease and Syphilis have been with us for hundreds if not thousands of years and there is absolutely no reason at all why low grade gene pool expression of these diseases is not deep down inside us all. Sitting there just waiting for an opportunity to take hold of our bodies through ageing, bodily damage or simply on the background of a previous disease invasion.

Now hey as I've said many times I'm no clinician but you would have thought by now that someone in the medical industry would have put one and one together and come out with two. But they haven't and the consequence of that is that we as society are lead to believe that when we've been diagnosed with Arthritis we have;

- Some form of overly complex condition.

- That there is no cure for us and we must live with it.

And

- There's only the steroid and/or anti-inflammatory approach we can take.

Well I think the only thing that's complicated about Arthritis is the insidious impact that the untreated disease has upon our ability to live life as we would choose. I don't think we need to believe that living with the condition is all that we can choose to do. Neither do I believe that just popping in anti-inflammatory tablets to mask the condition is the right or most effective way to move forward. I simply don't believe what the medics have to say on this condition or recommend in terms of its treatment. I believe that if we wish not to be held to ransom by a condition we must detach from the prejudices that surround that condition and be prepared to research and explore it further. You don't have to be silly here all you need to be is receptive to a whole host of new ideas and perceptions. But if you're unable to do that then your only option is to stick with the current orthodox views that might or might not be working for you.

Personally once I understood that the majority of medics that I elicited help from actually understood very little themselves. It became easy for me in that difficult position to accept that perhaps there's always more to explore about the originators of disease than a mere medic is willing to explore. My view now is:

- So what if you've been told you have arthritis, that doesn't prevent you from being tested privately to see if you have Lymes or any one of a hundred diseases!

- So what if you've been told you have arthritis, that doesn't prevent you from researching and exploring alternative treatments!

- So what if you've been told you have arthritis, that doesn't prevent you from trying under professional guidance a whole host of natural anti-bacterial, anti-viral and anti-inflammatory herbs!

But there is one thing for sure; if you let that disease expression take hold of your body by merely blocking its expression through high dose anti-inflammatory medications, then you will never be able to repair its damage. But then again it's your choice at the end of the day.

At the point I began to understand my pain I knew my life had changed

EXPLORING FIBROMYALGIA PRAGMATICALLY

Exploration Eleven

I live every day to the full now since I began to live again pain free

At the point I began to understand my pain I knew my life had changed

What is fibromyalgia? Well prior to being diagnosed with Lymes Disease I thought that I had it because fibromyalgia is a chronic condition that causes pain all over the body and I had that in excess. The condition in general manifests as intense and unrelenting pain that affects bands of tissue that connect bone to bone whilst directly and indirectly generating;

- Widespread pain.

- Fatigue.

- Depression.

- Extreme sensitivity to pain.

- Muscles stiffness.

- Tendons and ligaments.

I live every day to the full now since I began to live again pain free

The name fibromyalgia comes from the Latin word 'fibro' meaning fibrous tissues *tendons, ligaments*, 'my' meaning muscles, and 'algia' meaning pain.   Fibromyalgia used to be known as fibrositis, which literally means inflammation of the muscles and soft tissue. The condition was renamed fibromyalgia however after some studies found that there was no inflammation, or nerve injury. 'Hmmn no damage, absolute bloody rubbish' however that medical non experiencing conclusion was probably drawn by some numpty simply propelling their career.

The problem is that despite current medical dogma surrounding what this condition is and what this condition isn't, you can bet your entire bank account that at the point your body dips into fibromyalgia symptomology. The medical world will fail you, will write you off and label you as a neurotic. What's more there will be rounds of clap trap talked about sleep cycles, psychological predispositions and treatment options as puerile as treating a severed leg with a band aid.

What there will not be is unequivocal diagnostic or validated scientific rationale applied to your presenting symptoms, simply because the medical world continues to bark up the wrong trees with conditions of this nature. You see, main stream treatment of fibromyalgia is geared toward improving the quality of sleep and reducing pain by the suppression of the sufferer's symptoms but not solving the overall problem. Instead medications that boost your body's level of serotonin and norepinephrine neurotransmitters may be the only thing prescribed in low doses on the premise that they modulate sleep, pain, and immune system functions examples of which include:

- Amitriptyline.

- Cyclobenzaprine.

- Cymbalta.

At the point I began to understand my pain I knew my life had changed

At no point will you be tested for any underlying disease, nor will your clinical care team be in the slightest bit interested in exploring the potential of disease. Simply because fibromyalgia is incurable and is nothing more than a psychologically driven condition or at least that's current medical dogma prescriptively dictates.

But is fibromyalgia an incurable and psychologically driven condition? Well it might be if the medical industry were able to prove both statements but the stark answer is, they can't.

Therefore fibromyalgia is only classified as an incurable and psychologically driven condition because the medical industry has been unable to identify its root cause and therein lies the problem.

At the point that the medical industry can't prove the root cause of a condition, then the condition simply doesn't exist except for the handle it's given and the generic prequalification status that is assigned to it i.e. name: Fibromyalgia, originator of disease: a psychologically driven condition, end of story full stop.

But people with this condition endure almost insufferable pain, because they're unable to rest, to exercise, or do anything remotely normal and quite frankly it is pain beyond any other form of pain. It's unrelenting, it's the last thing a sufferer remembers before they fall asleep (if they're lucky enough to get some sleeps) and it's the first thing that greets them upon awakening.

It saps the life force from people, it lowers their emotions, restricts their capabilities and horizons; it is without any shadow of a doubt hell on earth. So the questions all Fibromyalgia sufferers need to ask themselves are:

(a)'Am I prepared to accept this diagnosis?'

And

(b) 'Am I prepared to endure this level of suffering without support or recovery?'

If the answers to those two simple questions are yes and yes, then you may as well stop reading this chapter and resign yourself to your fate, but if you're not prepared to accept that position then carry on reading and good for you.

At the point I began to understand my pain I knew my life had changed

So; having concluded that you're not prepared to accept your current diagnosis and prognosis then you're at least open to the potential of recovery. And when we are open to the potentials of recovery our energies are expansive not restrictive. With that mind set, anything and everything is possible and your road to understanding of the potential of recovery has just begun.

So now let's just take this a lit bit further. What other sorts of symptoms may we experience with fibromyalgia? Well we may experience:

- Facial pain, often as a result of neck, shoulder, or jaw muscle stiffness.

- Tingling, numbness, prickling, or burning sensations in your hands and feet *paresthesia.*

- Dry eyes, skin, or mouth.

- Irritable bowel syndrome.

- Painful testicles.

- Temperature control problems.

- Unusually painful menstruation cycles.

- Distorted or changes in vision.

- Noise sensitivity.

- Foggy, muggy thinking and forgetfulness.

I live every day to the full now since I began to live again pain free

- Anxiety.

- Depression.

So having already read some of the earlier chapters in this book let me ask you this, are there any alarm bells ringing for you in terms of synergistic health connections between fibromyalgia and:

- Lymes Disease?

- Adrenal insufficiency?

- Neurotoxin / biotoxin load?

- Hypothyroidism?

Well there should be because there can be absolutely no doubt that fibromyalgia is nothing more than presenting symptomology of a diseased state. It's not some incurable psychologically driven condition, its real, and it's the result of your body being under attack by some form of biological assailant which is having a profound effect upon your body's recovery and building blocks.

The only challenge you face now is accepting that position after years of suffering, after years and years of many unsuccessful treatments and after years of being told that it was you who was ultimately responsible for your condition.

At the point I began to understand my pain I knew my life had changed

You see; the psychological damage of unrelenting suffering and highly opinionated yet spectacularly unsuccessful treatment approaches erodes our ability at times to think out of the box. Partners, lovers, clinicians and colleagues have all written us off, they've all bought into the orthodox false truth and so at the point you begin to challenge their perceptions of your condition that is the very same point that you will unintentionally alienate yourself further. Simply because people just love to assign everything and everyone into nice neat little boxes, and they simply hate it and us if we dare to change their view of anything or anyone that they've previously assigned a view upon. That's just the way it is I'm afraid so all you can do is accept it and allow yourself to move on.

Now there is no point talking to any ignorant medic about anything I'm postulating here because that will expend high levels of your emotional, physical and spiritual resolve that you quite simply don't have at your disposal when battling with your symptoms. What you need to do is sit back, stay open, commit to your own personal research and decide if you're going to take your clinical investigation up to another level. If you decide to take that route, then you will need to look for:

- Bacteria impositions.

- Fungal impositions.

- Viral impositions.

Then you will need to;

- Qualify your mitochondrial function.

- Qualify your neuro / biotoxin load.

- Prepare yourself for the options that lay before you.

You see, it's all well and good to have a diagnosis postulated, but until we have the entire picture, it's impossible to qualify which is the originator and which is indicator of any of our chronic health expressions.

Effective treatment requires root cause analysis, anything less than that simply results in potential escalation or at best palliation without ultimate resolution of a presenting disease state expression.

Fibromyalgia is an eminently resolvable condition when the focus of attention in its treatment moves as far away from the suppression of symptoms and moves closer to removing its originators and cleaning and repairing our bodily systems. Because disease eradication and not simply symptom addressing must remain at all times your one and only goal.

To improve you must subject your bodily functions to responsible clinical investigations, you must accept that there are organic and biological agents at work and you must focus your attention upon finding out what they are and how you will transform your body from that diseased state. Accept and understand that simply root cause analysis and nothing more will help you heal yourself and your healing process has already begun.

Word of caution always work with professional supervision, do not embark upon anything you don't fully understand, keep both your heart and your mind open and for sure you'll find the answer to your fibromyalgia expression. Thereafter you can bin that name because the truth of the matter when all said and done is that fibromyalgia in whatever part that it's played in your life. Was really nothing more, than a medically manufactured condition designed only to absolve the incompetent of any sense of responsibility in relation to their failure of due diligence towards you in your care. Now how perverse is that when all said and done in terms of ethically amoral conduct.

I live every day to the full now since I began to live again pain free

```
        Mental ←·····················→        Karmic
          ↓                                     ↑
                      Fibromyalgia
    ┌──────────────→              ←──────────────┐
    │                                            │
 Disease              Accept Cause            Body System
 Lymes                     ↓                    Blood
 Chlamydia                                      Liver
 Aids ←───────────     Test For    ───────────→ Digestion
 HIV                       ↓                    Adrenals
 Herpes           ┌── Treat ←──┐               Thyroid
 Malaria          │      ↓      │               Thymus
 Sand Fly         │  Clean / Detox ←─┐          Parathyroid
 Candida          │      ↓          │           Pancras
 Malaria          │  Repair Systems │           Pituitary
 Bronchitis       │      ↓          │           Proteins
 Syphilis         │   Depression    │           Minerals
 Tuberculosis     │      ↓          │           Vitamins
 Toxins           │  Rest / Hydrate │           Enzymes
 etc              │      ↓          │           etc
                  │  Strengthen Body│
                  │      ↓          │
                  └──  Treat ───────┘
                          ↓
                     LIVE AGAIN
                          ↓
                        Treat
                          ↓
Challenge or Explore ← ENJOY LIFE → Challenge or Explore
```

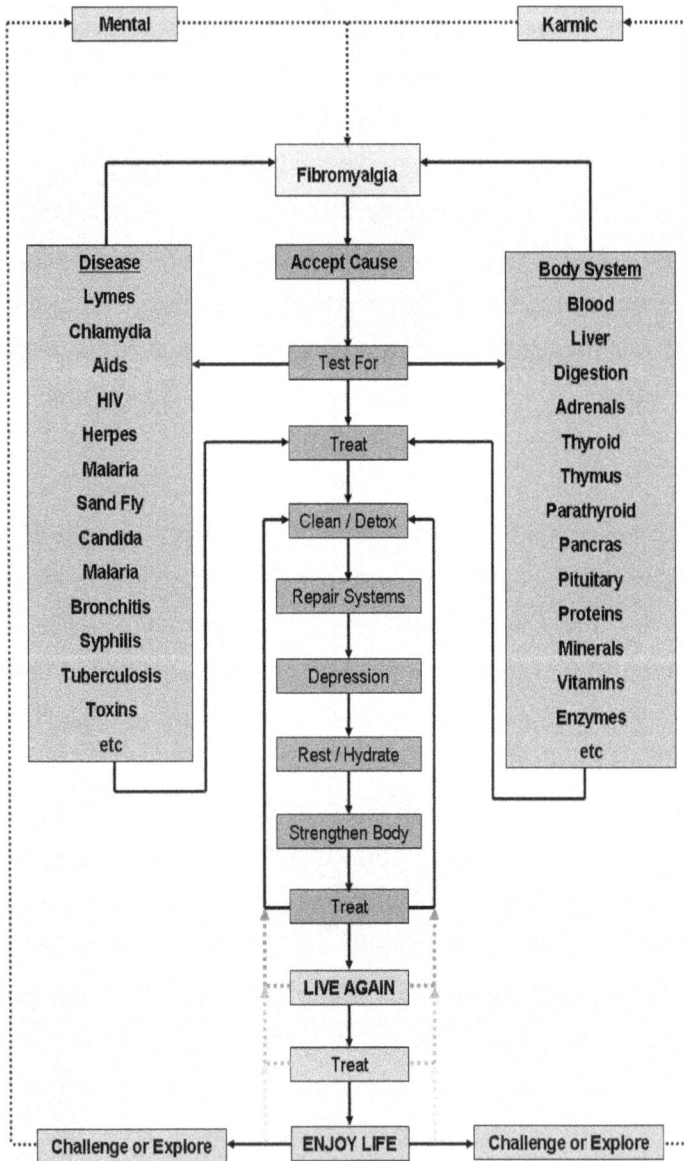

**Does a man move into a Fibromyalgia state because of the state of his mind or is he pushed
into that Fibromyalgia state because of the state of his body? – YOUR CHOICE !**

At the point I began to understand my pain I knew my life had changed

EXPLORING PERSONAL MIND ANGER PRAGMATICALLY

Exploration Twelve

At the point I began to understand my pain I knew my life had changed

You know I've encountered many many very special people in my life and I'm incredibly grateful for the interactions that I've had with them all. I've been blessed to meet fine tradesmen, carers, beggars, artists, clergymen, engineers, bus drivers, road sweepers, teachers, librarians, sportsmen etc., to name just a few. Each one special and unique in their own right, each one bringing something special to my life and yet I can count on one hand the medics I've met whom I would bestow the accolade of special upon.

Yet I make no secret of the fact that whilst I will be as gracious as circumstances dictate when interacting with members of the medical industry. I nevertheless have absolutely no respect for that industry or the views of those employed within it for unless I meet a medic who is able to speak or offer a service from a point of true expertise and I don't mean legitimized bullshit. Then I'm simply not interested in what any medic has to say, and I mean, I'm not interested in anything they have to say on health, politics or any major imposition on life.

You see, as far as I'm concerned they are the lowest of all mortal forms of life. The way these people conduct themselves, fail and abuse people in their care is a scandal and disgrace and for that I'm adamant that for their crimes against humanity they must pay a very heavy price, be that in this life or the next I really don't care. Until that happens I think its fine to explore in your head exactly what you would do to the rogues who've abused and failed you if you ever got the chance to deliver your own unique and personal retributions.

Now whilst some may say: *'Oh dear it's important for our souls and our recovery that we must let go of hatred and anger towards others'.* My answer is simply this, *'Explore that position again when you're tormented by a toxic liver, a toxic body and when every system and organ in your body has been damaged by an insidious bacteria, when it all could have been so easily prevented'* and then I would urge you to simply think your belief structures over again.

You see I personally believe that it's actually extremely healthy and positive to exercise your liver and brain anger. To explore just how far your emotions take you and what you think is suitable, punishment or not, for the suffering you've endured. Who knows, the very fact that you're prepared to explore those thoughts whilst accepting them for what they are, may just be an essential component of your recovery and a vital process that must not be ignored.

With that point of view in focus, I've had some lovely despicable thoughts about what I would like to do to the rogues who failed me. I so desperately want them to feel the level of pain that they create and perpetuate for people like me every minute of every day of their career. I've had thoughts of rounding all medics and their families up and transferring them to great football stadiums around the country.

At the point I began to understand my pain I knew my life had changed

Where I would strap the medics into chairs and make them watch their loved ones being torn apart without mercy by Hyenas. Now obviously that would take some time because there's only so much a Hyena can eat at any given time but that's okay, the longer the suffering for all concerned the better as far as I'm now concerned. You may ask why I chose Hyenas not lions, tigers, wolfs or bears, well it's because of all the big carnivores the Hyena is in my opinion the cruelest of them all. They don't waste energy killing their victims they simply rip them apart limb from limb. I think being eaten alive and enduring unbelievable suffering before death is fine for the sort of people that I have in mind.

Now of course and after a few years naturally there wouldn't be any family or loved ones left to brutalize, so I would turn my attention directly to the medics. At which point I really would enjoy playing mind games with them torturing them day after day for years. I would inject them with all sorts of substances and break the odd one or two limbs. There would be no quarter given, no repose on grounds of mercy.

But I might allow the odd one of two to read a few books on psychology if they felt it would help them deal or cope with their physical and emotional pain. I would inject some with Lymes Disease, some with HIV, some with syphilis and some with a blend of all three. But before all of that I would revel in playing games with their head and simply talk infinitum about a whole host of things I was planning to do.

I live every day to the full now since I began to live again pain free

The key in all my punishment regimes would be the generation of intolerable isolation, desolation and despair, creating a situation devoid of any humanistic sympathy or due diligence and care. In fact to replicate the culture that these rogues have rolled out on us for years, only in my regime there would be no 'DSBL's' written, no bullshit spoken and no postulation of care, my open and honest policy would be one of simple retribution and payback for the insidious lives that they'd lived.

Now I'm not sure if my anger towards the medical industry will ever subside but what matter that, all that I know is that I can't possibly allow my hatred of them to hold me back. I'm no longer their victim or some innocent that they can indiscriminately abuse, for I'm now 'Barry Hardy' the battle hardened medic hater who will delight in pursuing legal retribution and in due course regardless of whatever form or format that takes.

You see; I want everyone who's ever been chronically ill yet failed by the medical industry to realise and accept fully that they themselves were never to blame. In accepting that they, like me can exercise the demons that reside deep within us all after years of suffering. Because in accepting and not fighting our mind anger, I firmly believe that we're actually setting ourselves free. Simply because personal exploration as far as I'm concerned is nothing more than an intuitive expansive trait and if we choose to live in expansive state we very often leave our pain and suffering behind.

Now, let me make myself clear, I would never advocate actual violence against any medical service sector worker, rogues though they are by default. Nevertheless I certainly believe and therefore think that it's healthy and positive to accept and explore our brain and liver anger because it has a vital part to play in anyone's recovery.

My only footnote would be in closing this chapter is; go gentle into that vile place and never allow yourself to be completely consumed by your cruel thoughts, just accept them for what they are.

It really is okay to hate your medical abusers and accept that they are complete 'shits, cretins and clowns'. It's okay to hate their husbands, wives and kids for reaping great rewards from being associated with and/or to those rogues.

The only point I would make is turn that hatred into positive redress and legal action and don't let it just fester or simply evaporate away. Make your formal complaints if that's what you need to do for in doing so you will kick start a myriad of much needed karmic events.

Network with fellow mindsets and empower yourself in firm assurance that you're no longer that lone foot soldier that you'd lead yourself to believe you are, because at the point you empower your psyche to engage in seeking redress, you've morphed into a dynamic and cataclysmic particle of change.

That will prove to you once and for all, that you're a very real, dramatic, even majestic vanquisher of what is an insidious blight upon society i.e. our shockingly poor and unresponsive medical model, industry and the shits who work within it who are happy to destroy far too many peoples' lives.

At the point I began to understand my pain I knew my life had changed

EXPLORING ANALYTICAL TESTING PRAGMATICALLY

Exploration Thirteen

I live every day to the full now since I began to live again pain free

At the point I began to understand my pain I knew my life had changed

It's fair to say that some of us really go through the mill several times before our illness is finally diagnosed, yet at the point we're diagnosed we then hopefully via an effective treatment regime, can begin to make a substantive recovery from our presenting conditions. Sadly however, some of us actually never recover and that's primarily due to two reasons:

- Our condition is terminal.

- Or analytical sciences and clinical investigations are simply unable to detect a problem.

Ironically, during my baron chronic illness resolution days, whilst I was failed wholesale by UK analytical sciences and clinical investigations, I was diagnosed as terminally ill in the USA. How strange is that?

Well not that strange really when you scratch the surface of analytical sciences and clinical investigations in the UK. You see, the vast majority of tests, machines, and imaging devices that we have in the UK are not state of the art as the industry or our government would like us to believe. They're actually state of the ark. It's not until you actually analyse the state of that medical service sector that you find out just how bad things really are.

A situation compounded further by the front end medical cretins who request investigations and then either play a part or choose to abstain from interpolating any subsequent results objectively leaving us as the sufferer bemused.

I really don't think there can be anything worse than having a major health impediment and yet because of out dated and fundamentally flawed analytical sciences and clinical investigations no one can find anything wrong with you. At that point despite your intense suffering you're simply written off as a neurotic and the most alarming thing is that there is no difference either between the NHS and the private sector.

Time after time I've paid for very expensive consultations and tests and time after time some pompous, greedy, ignorant 'medical rogue' has said to me, 'actually there's nothing wrong with you your tests are normal Mr. Hardy' Followed by, 'have you considered psychiatric help?'

Equally in the NHS I've been abused in far too many situations by 'medical rogues' saying, 'Mr. Hardy there's absolutely nothing wrong with you it's all in your head' and their other favourite line, 'Mr. Hardy we can't keep on testing you why can't you just accept that you have a mental health issue?'

It is primarily because of all the rubbish and abuse I've had to endure that I advocate that we must take control of this situation. How dare some talentless, badly trained yet public sector worker say that the NHS can't keep testing me or anyone of us? I've / we've funded their bloody training, I / we've funded their bloody life styles and some of us have battled to preserve their bloody rotten industry from the ravages of Thatcherism. Boy do those 'charlatans' really make me angry.

At the point I began to understand my pain I knew my life had changed

You see, I really don't give a hoot if the NHS has to perform a thousand bloody tests upon me to find out what's wrong with me, that's what it's there for and therefore that's what it needs to do. Or it could certainly begin in the name of greater efficiencies, to look at the amount of money it's wasting on fundamentally flawed analytical sciences and clinical investigations and start bring its house in order.

Because if some clerical or 'clinical rogue' is assigning limits to the level of care that I can have from the NHS, then I for one now say let's have voluntary contributions to the NHS. Why should I a potential high earner pay ridiculous amounts of money to underwrite an industry that doesn't want to underwrite me when I need it? Yet it throws billions away on consultant's salaries and treats any chancer who decides to pop over to the UK for treatment.

Now hey I would never in a million years have thought that this working class lad from Woodhouse would ever have held such views towards the NHS. But having been exposed head on to all its woeful underperformance, ignorance and incompetence for years, I'm happy to voice my harsh views now. My belief now is that we need to bring this entire rotten industry crashing to its knees. So that as a nation we're able to build a clinical care service sector that is thorough, competitive; inspirational and world class and let's ditch the clap trap and rubbish of the past.

I live every day to the full now since I began to live again pain free

The problem with that vision is that the people who have suffered most from its shoddy service are unfortunately the ones with the lowest vitality, presence or voice. So before any of its victims can commit to campaigning for change they need to get well for only then can they hope to bring about change. But be under no illusion that dynamic changes quickly at the point our health returns. Unfortunately the road to recovery can be lonely, long and unrewarding at times and so until we reach our desired destination, its best for all chronically ill patients to focus solely upon regaining their health and leave the clinical reform campaign to better times.

Prior to our return to health however, let me give you a flavour of what happens in the normal psyche when we're experiencing a health condition and require analytical sciences and/or clinical investigations. We immediately make either a big or small deal of the fact that our condition is going to be subject to further scrutiny. Some of us may be worried that something dreadful may be found, whilst others may simply be happy if something could be found to enable us to be treated, recover and move on. I've always come from the school of thought, 'I hope they can find something so that I could move on'. I've never subscribed to worrying about there being something dreadfully wrong with me, because I only ever wanted solutions. I knew for years that I had something seriously wrong with me; I just didn't know what it was. If we don't know what's wrong with us then we can't ever hope to recover and in poor health, recovery must be our sole interest if we wish to regain some form of quality of life. Therefore we must commit to testing and analytical investigations and when the results come through, we must do our level best to acknowledge them and deal with them as appropriately as we're able to or at the very least, see fit.

At the point I began to understand my pain I knew my life had changed

So let's play the cycle through now, our test results come back and they're always in the standard form of:

- (a) Your tests are normal.

- (b) Hmmn, there is a slight problem but that might just be congenital.

- (c) You have bla bla bla bla.

- (d) You need to make an appointment to discuss your results.

Now to understand the ramifications of that feedback we need to look at the two generic psyches I discussed earlier i.e. big or small deal propensity. So let's look at the big deal psyche first:

(a) Results normal = maybe happy deep down and prepared to take whatever the medical representative says in terms of treatments etc., but may ham it up a bit when speaking to colleagues, family and friends.

(b) Result might be a congenital issue = may be worried deep down yet prepared to take whatever the medical representative says in terms of treatments etc. Might however blow the condition completely out of proportion and will certainly ham it up a bit when speaking to colleagues, family and friends.

(c) Result you have bla bla = may be extremely worried and also might blow the condition completely out of proportion until reassured by the medic, but will certainly ham it up a lot when speaking to colleagues, family and friends.

I live every day to the full now since I began to live again pain free

(d) Result you need a follow up appointment = extremely worried and will blow the condition completely out of proportion, because that brings the drama they crave into their life. As long as it's a safe and controllable drama that's fine, should it however not be a safe drama then they will start off being publicly very brave and then simply implode putting tremendous pressure on anyone in close proximity.

So let's look at the small deal psyche now:

(a) Results normal = maybe confused deep down but prepared to take to some extent whatever the medical representative says.

(b) Result might be a congenital issue = may be worried but certainly interested in the result more from a clinical perspective than a sensationalist perspective.

(c) Result you have bla bla = may be worried but happy that there is something to discuss, but will need answers.

(d) Result you need a follow up appointment = worried until they understand what's wrong with them, but once they know they just get their heads down with it and are normally stronger than the people around them, who sometimes fall to pieces.

Now look it doesn't really matter what personality type you fall into. The key to returning to optimum health is ensuring that you're either prepared to be driven or you're prepared to drive the situation. Either way your focus must be upon achieving optimum health, because if you're not experiencing optimum health then you need to understand why; assuming that is that optimum health is your real goal. I've postulated that we must all examine if optimum health is our real goal, and I raise that challenging point because whilst some people will say optimum health is their goal. You only have to talk or listen to them to understand that they are indeed lost or closed to the potential of optimum health. That is because some people really do like being ill, because in being ill they:

- Have the crutch they need.

- Don't need to compete.

- Can offload all their personal issues at the door of their illness or disease.

At the point I began to understand my pain I knew my life had changed

Now there is absolutely no crime in that, save to say, if a man does not wish to help himself, then perhaps help is not what he needs. You see there are no secrets to optimum health save for a desire to have optimum health, yet within that expectation and desire there are many levels of acceptance and abstinence. Only we as individuals have the sole right to make the value judgments that best meet our desires and needs.

My personal expectations have always been to secure a quality of life that is free from physical impediments and diseased states. Because of that I've mapped a holistic yet pragmatic approach to this process on the next page, now whilst it may initially look complex when you first see it. Just take time to follow some of the evolution and iteration loops from your own perspective and you'll find that it caters precisely for whichever mind set you are.

I live every day to the full now since I began to live again pain free

The only secret to having good health is ones personal determination to have good health

At the point I began to understand my pain I knew my life had changed

During my pre-diagnostic state my only abstinences were to reject wholesale any and all forms of clap trap or ignorantly manufactured dogma articulated to distract me from my goal. I advocate only this that in the pursuit of optimum health we all must accept that we alone are the responsible party for driving the process of recovery through diagnosis. For without our input, there is no other form of input worthy of comment and therefore no reasonable probability of making any form of sustainable recovery.

Yet whilst that is, or can be, a very difficult path for some of us to walk alone, in reality it's the only path that delivers access to clarity, understanding, effective treatment and recovery. It is by default however; a process of two stages, the first stage is the stage where we are in essence ignorant and unable to make progress because we rely completely upon false testing, consultations and investigations which have little if any merit. I've mapped that process for you on the next page, because once we understand all the loops in the process, it is no longer a mystery and can indeed become that defining point from which we all move forward.

I live every day to the full now since I began to live again pain free

```
                          ┌──────────────┐
                          │   Symptoms   │
                          └──────┬───────┘
                                 ↓
                          ┌──────────────┐ ┐
                    ┌ ─ ─>│   Research   │ │
                    ┆     └──────┬───────┘ │
                    ┆            ↓         │
                    ┆     ┌──────────────┐ │
                    ┆     │     Test     │ │  Stage one
                    ┆     └──────┬───────┘ │
                    ┆            ↓         │
                    ┆     ┌──────────────┐ │
                    ┆     │ Result Normal│ │
                    ┆     └──────┬───────┘ │
                    ┆            ↓         │
                    ┆     ┌──────────────┐ │
                    └ ─ ─ ┤  Frustration │ ┘
                          └──────────────┘
                          ┌──────────────┐ ┐
                          │     Test     │ │
                          └──────┬───────┘ │
                                 ↓         │
                          ┌──────────────┐ │
                          │Result Abnormal│ │
                          └──────┬───────┘ │
                                 ↓         │
                          ┌──────────────┐ │
                          │    Treat     │ │
                          └──────┬───────┘ │
                                 ↓         │
                          ┌──────────────┐ │  Stage two
                          │     Test     │ ┆ ─ ─ ─ ─┐
                          └──────┬───────┘ │        ┆
                    ┌────────────┼────────┐│        ┆
                    ↓            ↓        ↓│        ┆
           ┌──────────────┐  ┌──────────────┐       ┆
           │Result Normal │  │Result Abnormal│      ┆
           └──────┬───────┘  └──────┬───────┘       ┆
                  └────────┬────────┘                ┆
                           ↓                         ┆
                    ┌──────────────┐                 ┆
                    │   Research   ┆ ─ ─ ─ ─ ─ ─ ─ ─>┆
                    └──────┬───────┘                 ┆
                           ↓                         ┆
                    ┌──────────────┐                 ┆
                    │    Treat     ┆ ─ ─ ─ ─ ─ ─ ─ ─ ┘
                    └──────┬───────┘
                           ↓
                    ┌──────────────┐
                    │    Health    │
                    └──────────────┘
```

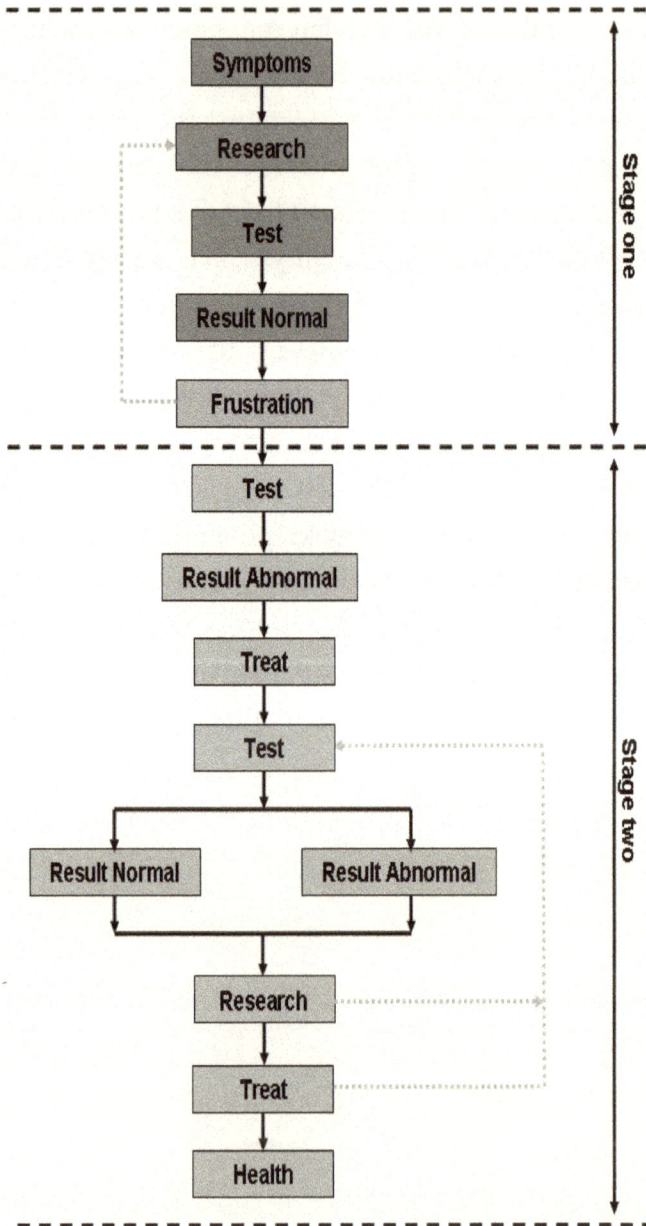

Ignore the doubters who say you can't keep on testing you can and you must

At the point I began to understand my pain I knew my life had changed

The second stage is where we take ownership of the intellect responsibility for substantiating our underlying condition or conditions. It is the point that we start unravelling our health mysteries, that remarkable point where we see the medical industry and those who support it for what and who they really are.

Both stages are incredibly difficult because they are both encountered when we have lower than normal vitality. Stage one will invariably consist of a 90% - 10% NHS and private involvement whereas 'stage two' will be the complete opposite i.e. 10% - 90% NHS and private involvement.

Therefore there are significant cost implications required of those attempting to return to a position of optimum health. Some of that money will be wasted and some of it will be money well spent. There is no right or wrong course of action to take, all we can ever be is true to ourselves and whilst we can't beat the obscene and perverse nature of the medical industry. We can get better through our own efforts and eventually realise our dreams if only we're prepared to drive the testing and analysis until a reflective diagnosis has been achieved. In my particular situation stage one of my investigation process consisted of nothing more than the following fundamentally flawed investigations below:

- 3 Liver enzyme tests.

- 3 Thyroid tests.

- 1 MRI.

- 1 CT.

- 1 X-ray investigation.

I live every day to the full now since I began to live again pain free

The conclusions drawn from them were that I was fine and had nothing wrong with me except for mental health issues, time and time again. Whereas my stage two self funded investigations included:

- 5 MRI's.

- 2 MRA's.

- 4 CAT scans.

- 2 CT's.

- 60+ blood tests and bodily function analysis, tests and examinations.

- 9 Caloric Tests.

- 3 Hearing Tests.

- 9 ENG Tests.

- Two Neurosurgical procedures.

- 180+ clinical consultations all around the world plus travel and accommodation.

- Plus thousands of hours research on the internet long before cheap broad band, etc.

- In summation personal traceable costs in excess of 300K.

At the point I began to understand my pain I knew my life had changed

The result of my tenacity in the face of unbelievable odds was that I was eventually diagnosed with:

- Chronic late stage Lymes Disease.

- Chronic mitochondria failure.

- Chronic liver disease.

- Chronic adrenal insufficiency.

- And an extremely rare genetic yet organic anomaly resulting in a Posterior Inferior Cerebella Artery insulting my vestibular bundle and brain stem left side. *Note this condition still imposes great suffering upon me every minute of every day and that's why just putting my thoughts onto paper is such an almighty affair.*

Now look, the point I'm making is that there are far too many issues surrounding our poor medical investigation model and too many issues surrounding outdated machines and devices being postulated as state of the art diagnostic tools. How many of us actually know until we are faced with horrendous medical conditions just how bad the equipment and techniques used to analyse our bodies truly are through-out the nhs because if we did I'm sure our own dogs of war would be unleashed.

How many of us have been for an MRI scan and been told that everything is normal, when in reality the MRI scanner being used is:

- Badly designed and maintained?

- Outdated and malfunctioning?

- An expensive piece of scrap metal?

- Operated by people who don't give a shit.

Now we all know the difference between top and low end motoring in terms of performance etc, but very few of us know that the same is the case in the medical industry. You see, in the push to kid us all into thinking our health is safe in their hands, NHS trusts all around the country installed sub standard equipment which in the majority of instances are nothing more than token gestures in terms of world class clinical investigation tools. The differences are so wide in terms of performing basic functions that it's like giving one man a set of binoculars and another an electron microscope to analyse the same bacteria, now that would be simply ridiculous wouldn't it?

Well the truth is, the state of our nation's clinical diagnostic tools is not simply ridiculous, it's actually a disgrace and we the front end users or mugs are the ones paying the highest price. We're sent for diagnostic investigations, the results come back normal and the result of that is, no further line of investigation undertaken despite the fact that your condition may continue to decline.

Simply because a shit piece of equipment operated by people who don't give a shit has indicating that you have no problem or in point of fact is unable to detect the problem you have. Now I sincerely hope that my observations through suffering and personal wasted expense has set off some alarm bells deep within you because those alarm bells need to resonate with us all as a society each and every day because we need this resolved not next year or next month I would respectfully suggest but tomorrow and it must happen before lunch time at the very latest.

Because I advocate that when and where there is evidence to suggest that the instruments, techniques, systems and protocols used to support clinical investigations are incapable of investigating with the degree of enquiry that we need, then we need to:

- Challenge the results.

- Find suitable systems etc, which can perform to the level and standard of integrity that we require.

You see, I'm no solo foot soldier here, millions of us are being written off every year by fundamentally flawed medical investigations, consultations and tests. So if you truly desire optimum health, you're going to have to fight for it with all your intellect, strength and might. You're going to have to:

- Ignore the personal and clinical prejudices that you encounter.

- You're going to have to spend money that you may not have.

- You're going to have to prove your condition yourself.

I live every day to the full now since I began to live again pain free

Because if you think for one moment that the state, the NHS or our private medical health circus will resolve anything more than a superficial health impediment then your sadly mistaken because they won't. Only you can drive this stage two part of your pursuit of disease expression reflective diagnosis, because in reality there really only is you who truly gives a damn. So to help keep you upbeat and focused during that process I've mapped a very simple process approach plan for you below.

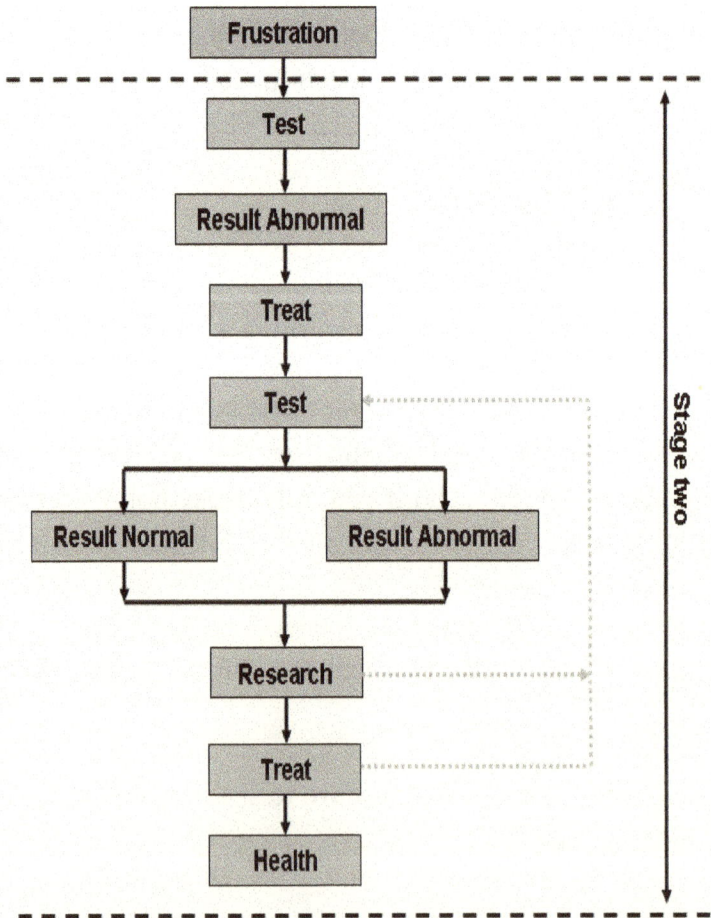

```
                    ┌─────────────────┐
                    │   Frustration   │
                    └────────┬────────┘
─ ─ ─ ─ ─ ─ ─ ─ ─ ─ ─ ─ ─ ─ ┼ ─ ─ ─ ─ ─ ─ ─ ─ ─ ─ ─ ─ ─ ┐
                    ┌────────▼────────┐                   │
                    │      Test       │                   │
                    └────────┬────────┘                   │
                    ┌────────▼────────┐                   │
                    │ Result Abnormal │                   │
                    └────────┬────────┘                   │
                    ┌────────▼────────┐                   │
                    │     Treat       │                   │
                    └────────┬────────┘                   │
                    ┌────────▼────────┐                   │
                    │      Test       │·····              │
                    └────────┬────────┘    :              S
              ┌──────────────┴──────────────┐             t
      ┌───────▼───────┐          ┌───────────▼───────┐    a
      │ Result Normal │          │  Result Abnormal  │    g
      └───────┬───────┘          └───────────┬───────┘    e
              │                  ┌───────────▼───────┐    
              └──────────────────│     Research      │····w
                                 └───────────┬───────┘    o
                                 ┌───────────▼───────┐    │
                                 │     Treat         │····│
                                 └───────────┬───────┘    │
                                 ┌───────────▼───────┐    │
                                 │     Health        │    │
                                 └───────────────────┘    │
─ ─ ─ ─ ─ ─ ─ ─ ─ ─ ─ ─ ─ ─ ─ ─ ─ ─ ─ ─ ─ ─ ─ ─ ─ ─ ─ ─ ┘
```

Ignore the doubters who say you can't keep on testing you can and you must

At the point I began to understand my pain I knew my life had changed

So that when you're at the other end of your health recovery campaign you can then speak from a platform of assurance, confidence and righteousness. You can challenge the integrity of those who failed you, ignored or abused you, because at that point you're more than an equal for anyone who would choose to play games with you because you're able to ask with assurance:

- Why are we as a nation wasting so much money on fundamentally flawed tests etc., whilst writing people off with impunity?

- Why are some of us, with a desire to be well, having to self research, self fund and self acquire best in class medical and clinical investigations outside the UK?

- Where is the medical establishment when we need it?

- Who within our current appalling medical service sector ranks can dare to defend this level of clinical and administrated incompetence?

I live every day to the full now since I began to live again pain free

There really is only one way to ensure that you get through your health predicaments and that is to take control of your stage two process whilst ensuring you stay in total control of your entire health optimisation process re: below.

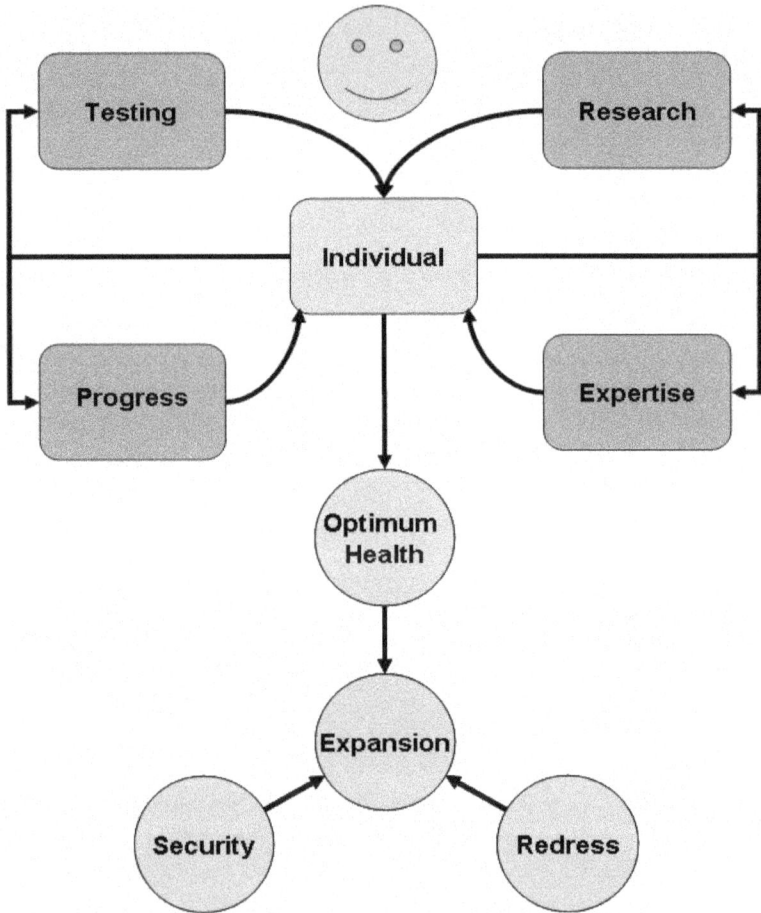

Taking Individual Control of All Health Related Processes

At the point I began to understand my pain I knew my life had changed

Exploring analytical testing options pragmatically

Exploration Fourteen

At the point I began to understand my pain I knew my life had changed

I've made great play throughout this book of the need for effective testing and re-testing if necessary, to enable effective diagnosis of underlying diseased states. Yet whilst those tests can take many forms including: imaging and bodywork. I believe that the key to identifying the root cause of any chronic condition begins with effective blood and biochemical marker analysis. The clinic that I used for my detailed blood analysis via my private GP Dr. Sarah Myhill referrals was 'Biolab Medical Unit UK'.

Biolab Medical Unit is a; medical referral laboratory specializing in nutritional and environmental medicine which is located in the heart of the West End of London. They are a nutritional biochemistry laboratory measuring vitamin and mineral levels, toxic metals, other biochemical levels that are related to the availability of vitamins, minerals and other nutrients. They have an extensive range of profiles for assessing the effects of twenty-first century lifestyles on our bodies and are dedicated to assisting doctor's sort out their patients' problems in a way that does not rely on drugs as a first line of treatment. Biolab apply modern scientific laboratory analytical methods to establish what imbalances there are in the bodies of those who are suffering ill-health or non-optimum health, so that these imbalances may be addressed via nutritional and non-drug means, with the aim of achieving good health or, at least, improving the quality of life and minimizing suffering.

I would therefore suggest that it's worth visiting their website at www.biolab.co.uk/ for a more detailed overview of their services, staff and publications etc. However please note that Biolab Medical Unit (UK) is a referral unit and will only perform tests requested by practitioners registered with;

- The General Medical Council.

I live every day to the full now since I began to live again pain free

- The General Dental Council.

- The General Osteopathic Council.

- The General Chiropractic Council.

All test reports will be sent to your practitioner as Biolab will not enter into direct discussions with you about your results, although they are happy to discuss their findings in relation to your tests with your practitioner. It's important to note that I have absolutely no commercial, professional or personal arrangement with Biolab Medical Unit or any other analytical service provider. Furthermore those services providers will be completely unaware of my personal use of their services or my recommendation of their services. I would nevertheless strongly urge any individual suffering from a chronic health condition and wishing to undergo private blood investigations etc., to discuss their case with their medical/clinical service provider and request that they enter into discussions with respective analytical service providers such as Biolab. But be under no illusion that you may find that an uphill battle because medics in general traditionally poo poo anything that deviates from their own ignorant perspectives. If that is the outcome of your discussions then you have only three choices open to you:

(a) Stay with your current service provider.

(b) Secure more appropriate service support.

Or

(c) Give up completely on life.

At the point I began to understand my pain I knew my life had changed

Ultimately as the masters of our own health and happiness we must make the choices we feel are best for us and in that we must be prepared to stand or fall, live or die by the choices we choose to make.

I live every day to the full now since I began to live again pain free

At the point I began to understand my pain I knew my life had changed

EXPLORING YOUR CURRENT
DIAGNOSIS PRAGMATICALLY

Exploration Fifteen

At the point I began to understand my pain I knew my life had changed

So; you've read my highly opinionated postulations in terms of the originators and drivers of chronic illness expression, the question now is are you up for testing your historical perceptions. If so let's explore that receptivity in this final chapter.

Do you know there is one sure fire thing about anyone suffering from chronic illness expression including Fibromyalgia and that is; sufferers will do and take anything they can to remove it from their life. The majority in the end resort to a whole raft of escapist options because living in their body is simply beyond mortal endurance at times. It's not untypical for a sufferer of Fibromyalgia to indulge and self indulge in a wide range of escapist pursuits some of which include:

- Exercise.
- Deviant acts.
- Drugs.
- Cigarettes.
- Alcohol.
- Orthodox medication.
- Herbal supplements.
- Homeopathy.

And even

- Suicide attempts.

Whilst others commit to

- Suicide completions.

I live every day to the full now since I began to live again pain free

Such is the suffering of those, experiencing unrelenting, Fibromyalgia that for most their only constant thought is that of finding some how or some way of detaching themselves from its grasp. As a former chronic illness sufferer, I know only to well the depth of despair that chronic illness can push you into when there is not a treatment, a medication, a supplement, an activity or self destruct approach that does not remove your major presenting symptoms. I truly know what it's like to live in a body when NOTHING and I mean NOTHING even remotely diminishes the impact of chronic illness upon your entire being. Nevertheless I'm stating firmly for the record that it's possible to lower chronic illness expression rapidly. In fact it's possible to feel better than you've ever felt in your life before, because at the point you address the underlying cause of your illness your recovery profile picks hitherto unthinkable momentum. Yet the approach that I prescribe is unlike any of the majority of orthodox options you may have encounter before because it does not include:

- Self beasting through Psychoanalysis.

Or

- Detachment though 'Somnolence' inducing concoctions.

Or even

- A combination of both ridiculous approaches.

At the point I began to understand my pain I knew my life had changed

You see, Raphael's Treatment Protocol RTP is based upon looking at chronic illness expression i.e. Fibromyalgia objectively and doing your utmost to uncover via root cause analysis the physical generator and/or generators of chronic illness expression before even looking at treating the symptoms of that disease generated diseased state. That is not to say that the sufferer is left in purgatory as is the case with current treatment approaches. Because the diminishment of negative symptom expression within hours is the short term goal of RTP, and that I may add is not some grandiose statement without substance because in reality it will be proven as fact. You see; if your original and/or presenting symptoms are the derivative of disease expression, which there is a great possibility that they are; then very simple, very effective and very safe bodily testing will prove that to you.

Thereafter RTP focuses upon the sustainability of underlying disease eradication whilst supporting the body through effective and re-energized removal of all associated toxic loads from the body. Note however that there are no ridiculous detox regimes in the RTP, no regimes of excessive supplement ingestion, but there is a need for whole body analysis and with that the chronic illness sufferer must accept there is an initial cost.

Extract Summary from the Raphael Treatment Protocol

1. You must have access to and be supervised by a suitably qualified practitioner.

2. You must NOT stop any treatment protocol you're currently undertaking until your analysis results have been compiled.

3. You must be prepared to accept that you will have to pay for several highly specilaised blood and bodily function tests including:

    i. Mitochondria Analysis.
    ii. Viral Analysis.
    iii. Chlamydia Analysis.
    iv. Lymes Disease Analysis.
    v. Syphilis Analysis.
    vi. Fungal Analysis.
    vii. Methylation Analysis.
    viii. Sulphanation Analysis.
    ix. Thyroid Analysis.

    And

    x. A 24 hour Saliva Adrenal Function test.

4. You must be prepared to look objectively at your results with your practitioner and understand exactly what's happening and/or going on in your body.

At the point I began to understand my pain I knew my life had changed

5. You must be prepared to undertake supervised treatment regimes designed to:

    i.   Quash any microorganism disease states.
    ii. Support and energize any diseased organ states.
    iii. Support your bodies detoxing capabilities.

6. Monitor your body at every stage of your treatment protocol because as covered in the TBS chapter it's important to know where you're at.

7. Above all be gentle with yourself because the road to recovery is full of ups and downs during the process of disease eradication, toxin removal and whole body system re-energization.

Be under no illusion that at the point you begin to address any underlying disease states and commence the process of bio/lipo toxin removal from your body you will begin to feel much better almost immediately. Thereafter windows of freedom from chronic illness expression will become more frequent until chronic illness expression is nothing more than far a distant episode from your past. Now look I'm not naive to think that anyone reading this chapter will fully understand the point I'm making about my alternative approach to chronic illness eradication. But there is a very simple test that anyone suffering from Fibromyalgia expression can do if they wish to explore a new way of understanding their condition and I qualify that for you on the next page.

I live every day to the full now since I began to live again pain free

Take a small quantity of the suggested products re: below over let's say one to four days. The products I'm referring to are natural yet highly potent and they can be bought online or from any good health food store. All the products I'm about to suggest are antimicrobial, antibacterial and anti-inflammatory which means that they will immediately kill foreign invaders whilst reducing initially some of any directly or indirectly associated inflammation. They are:

- One tea spoon of Higher Nature 'MSM organic Sulphur Crystals' in water morning and night.

Or

- 2-5 drops NutraMedix 'Samento' in water morning and night.

Or

- 2-5 drops NutraMedix 'Cumanda' in water morning and night.

Or

- 2-5 drops Higher Nature 'Citricidal' Grapefruit Seed Liquid Extract in water morning and night.

It should be noted that I have absolutely no commercial or clinical/medical arrangement with either Higher Nature or NutraMedix including any other directly or indirectly associated party. I'm merely citing their products simply because I found them to work well for me.

At the point I began to understand my pain I knew my life had changed

If you have an underlying disease which is responsible and/or contributing to your chronic illness expression then the result of taking small doses of the suggested products should be;

1. An immediate lifting in mood and may even move your mood slightly into a hyper or manic mode.

And

2. A reduction in bodily tension and pain and in some instance tension and pain may simply disappear.

However

3. The sufferer's mood will be drastically lowered again within a 8 / 12 hour window and all associated pain will increase with additional pain being generated in new and strange locations.

Now the reason all that happens time after time is because that is the standard Herxheimer Reaction (HR) that people with chronic disease states incur at the point they begin to address their diseased state. It's a toxic reaction generated in the body by toxins being released from dead or decaying parasites, fungus, viruses, bacteria or other pathogens. As these toxins circulate in our body, it is not uncommon to experience flu-like symptoms including headache, joint and muscle pain, body aches, sore throat, general malaise, sweating, chills, nausea or other symptoms. This is normal and indicates that parasites, fungus, viruses, bacteria or other pathogens are being effectively killed off.

The biggest battle we all face in recovering from disease expression via RTP is dealing with the HR in a way that enables us to function and ensure that we can continue to medicate and support our bodies through what is a truly hellish situation. I myself have arrived at that point now because after years of self treating and suffering I've found the formula that allows me to kill my bodily invaders whilst supporting my defective detox capabilities via a number of gentle treatment protocols not least of which includes the use of a far infrared sauna daily. But you can read more about that in my book *Raphael's Treatment Protocol*.

At the point I began to understand my pain I knew my life had changed

Now there is one further important point I need to make here in relation to the support of chronic illness suffers who are clearly experiencing some degree of endocrine system insufficiency and that is I completely agree with the medication of small doses of hormones in terms of:

1. Hydrocortisol and/or prednisolone to support the adrenals, *which can be purchased online without a prescription.*

And

2. Synthetic Armour to support the thyroid, *which can be purchased online without a prescription.*

So whilst pompous medics will cry foul on that matter and cite my support of such medications as evidence of my cavalier and ludicrous approach to wellness. All I can say is that in controlled and supervised dosage both medication offer far greater whole body health benefits than many well known prescription medications that are given out willy nilly. In fact they are probably less dangerous when handled with integrity than:

- Alcohol.

- Cigarettes.

- High fat foods.

And

I live every day to the full now since I began to live again pain free

- Controlled substances such as:

  I.   Crack cocaine.

  II.   Heroine.

  III. Marijuana etc.

All off which can be purchased with ease and consumed in completely irresponsibly fashions, all imposing greater harm onto already impoverished capabilities of sufferers with any form of chronic illness. All appear to be addictive and whilst some have a more direct impact upon specific organs, i.e. lungs, brain and liver. Unfortunately cocaine, heroine and marijuana carry a much deadlier addictive tendency and can even damage many areas in the brain not least of which includes Gaba receptors and associated neuro-networks leading to emotional/psychological complications.

Now look I've sort of laboured that point for one very specific reason, and that is if your tests prove you're suffering from adrenal insufficiency there is absolutely no way that a medic will provide you with small dose endocrine system support and so at that point your way forward is entirely up to you. Personally however I say stay well clear of the cigarettes, alcohol, high fat foods, cocaine, heroine and marijuana because they are only for people who've given up on life, so if you've chosen life which I hope you have then cast your net further and explore where you can find the endocrine help and support that you need.

I really get the hump when I hear 'luddite' medics rattling on about the dangers of endocrine system support and I do so because those very same 'charlatans' every day of their career abuse people in their care by default. On top of that they're only to happy to hand out in buckets or skips whichever is your choice, prescriptions for a whole host of side effect riddle concoctions. The very same concoctions that immediately place you in the:

- Psychiatric treatment trap, with all is shortfalls and associated medical/clinical abuse loops.

    And

- Compromise your body's recovery processes further by their highly toxic effects upon your methylation and sulphanation processes............arrrrrrrrrrr they make me so angry.

Let me be very clear here I'm in no way advocating that anyone suffering from chronic illness expression should walk away from the supervision and/or treatment protocols they're currently committed to. But what I am saying is that there is a need for a change in perceptions in and about the origin of chronic illness expression and my only hope is that at the very least my postulations enable some form of educated debate. No one should have to live with irresolvable chronic illness it is neither a karmic lesson nor an opportunity to grow. Chronic illness is nothing more than an insidious blight upon our lives and so no matter which way we or anyone from the medical/clinical industry chooses to look at it. The expression of chronic illness in society at large needs to be removed from our society and psyche completely and Amen.

If you do nothing else for the rest of the day after you've read this book I implore you to explore what I have to say from an educated and considered perspective and above all things be gentle with yourself and your body because at the end of the day, that's all we really have at our disposal. May your god and the power of your own force now take you to the place and space within your inner health where you need to go! A place that I hope now presents to you day after day; mortal beauty, hope, inspiration and love.

At the point I began to understand my pain I knew my life had changed

AUTHORS NOTES

I live every day to the full now since I began to live again pain free

At the point I began to understand my pain I knew my life had changed

Personal Insight and Ownership

I'm aware that I've scared and troubled many people in the past with my ability to: analyse, condemn, congratulate and even poke fun at myself in the pursuit of reality and my own personal progression. I'm a very big believer that personal insight and personal ownership of all our mortal endeavours is the key to a truly considered life. Therefore if the tone, substance and/or in-depth of personal expression or certain aspects of my personal life are too much for any of my readers. I would respectfully suggest that perhaps its time for them to stop reading and start writing, for the expression of repression certainly offers release as far as I understand, from the tension we all as mortals appear to manufacture with ease.

Medics and the Medical/Clinical World

The medical world is full of humans each with their own unique gifts, skills and personal flaws and it's because the medical world is full of mortals and not earth God's that they fail us so badly day after day. But don't just sit back any longer when you're abused, let down or failed by anyone in the medical/clinical world. Sue them and bring them and their industry to account if you desire, for in doing so you will not only help yourself via the pursuit of redress, but indirectly you'll play a very big part in helping the entire human race.

I live every day to the full now since I began to live again pain free

The Great Psychological Bluff and Scandal

If we allow others to cloud our realities in terms of who we are and what we're actually experiencing with inappropriate postulations about the state of our psychology, be under no illusion we fail ourselves completely at every conceivable level. On matters of psychology when pursuing well-being, listen to your antagonists but choose not to hear when you're being written as another psychological basket case. Because I'm confident you'll discover if you test your body thoroughly, that it's your body that's at fault not your emotions or mind. At that point all psychological assertions can be met head on as you pursue a meaningful life.

Eminently Solvable Conditions

When you're health conditions are being fudged and written off as illnesses that have only names with no treatment or resolution options open or offered to you to help you get by or simply cope. You really have only two options open to you and that is to stick with what you've got if that's all you can do or you can test and test until your condition or conditions are identified. We are all the sole guardians of our own mortality; therefore we can either relinquish our responsibility to the uncaring and obscene or we can fight for what is our mortal right, the right to decency and an acceptable quality of life.

At the point I began to understand my pain I knew my life had changed

Depression Expression

There is no insanity at all in depression expression save only for the sheer depth of suffering its victims incur. Because the reality is that depression expression can be eradicated in days, not weeks, months or years when the physical generators, precursors and accelerators of depression expression are treated and removed. All that is needed is a shift in perceptions, a position significantly enhanced by holistic treatment results.

Stressful Resolution

Whilst the majority of us have experienced some degree of stress at some point in our life, very few of us realise that it's so predictable, so treatable and so recoverable from, hence nothing whatsoever for us all to get stressed about. Once you understand the dynamics, your stress levels will fall and at that point you will wonder why you allowed yourself to get so stressed in the first place or indeed at all.

Wellness

There is no great secret to wellness over and above understanding the root cause of any decline from wellness into un-wellness. But that root-cause analysis is not determined by non intrusive subjective analysis, because it can only be determined by holistic, scientific testing and analysis. Anything less than that is mere supposition, supposition however has never cured anyone or created a state of considered wellbeing, but it has forced many poor mortals like you, me and us, to give up completely on the idea of a satisfying mortality. But no longer yeah?

I live every day to the full now since I began to live again pain free

Divine or Higher Force

We all at some point need someone or something to pray to, no matter what race or creed we originate from. But the reality is when all said and done, we all as mortals are the only living beings able to solve complex mortal mysteries, so whilst it's okay I suspect to offer up prayers. I think it best that we all put our faith in ourselves and the endeavours of our fellow men.

At the point I began to understand my pain I knew my life had changed

WEB SITES YOU MAY WISH TO EXPLORE

The information provided here is for research only; no responsibility will be accepted for the scope or content of any of these web sites.

1. www.doctormyhill.co.uk

2. www.biolab.co.uk/

3. www.thyroiduk.org/

4. www.nutramedix.com

5. www.mickeltherapy.com

6. www.moodcure.com/

7. www.reikifed.co.uk/

8. www.thyroidtears.co.uk/

9. www.paulocoelho.com/ *(My favourite Author)*

OTHER BOOKS BY BARRY HARDY

Further personal insight and self help books written by Barry Hardy in relation to Raphael's Legacy include:

Raphael Treatment Protocol
Stress at Close Quarters
Anxiety at Close Quarters
Exploring Fluid Normality
Arthritis at Close Quarters
Depression at Close Quarters
Lymes Disease at Close Quarters
Manic Depression at Close Quarters
Gulf War Syndrome at Close Quarters
Toxic Body Syndrome at Close Quarters
Myalgic Encephalopathy at Close Quarters
Chronic Fatigue Syndrome at Close Quarters
Obsessive Compulsive Disorder at Close Quarters

You can purchase any of these books at www.barryhardy.com

At the point I began to understand my pain I knew my life had changed

DECENCY WARNING

This warning is repeated and placed at the back of this book because if you're like my daughter you're sure to start at the back of this book and I certainly don't wish to offend any back book readers either. Therefore please don't read this book if you are easily offended by:

- Strong views.
- Strong language.
- Grammatical inconsistencies and/or poor grammar.

Or

- Personal experiences and perceptions expressed freely.

I live every day to the full now since I began to live again pain free

Personal Notes

At the point I began to understand my pain I knew my life had changed

Personal Notes

I live every day to the full now since I began to live again pain free

Personal Notes

At the point I began to understand my pain I knew my life had changed

Personal Notes

I live every day to the full now since I began to live again pain free

Personal Notes

At the point I began to understand my pain I knew my life had changed

Personal Test Results

I live every day to the full now since I began to live again pain free

Personal Test Results

Personal Treatment Notes

Personal Treatment Notes

Personal Treatment Notes

I live every day to the full now since I began to live again pain free

Personal Treatment Notes

At the point I began to understand my pain I knew my life had changed

www.ingramcontent.com/pod-product-compliance
Lightning Source LLC
Chambersburg PA
CBHW021228090426
42740CB00006B/433